SECRET CONVERSATIONS WITH INTERNET MILLIONAIRES

How to Make Money Online with an Internet Marketing Business

ROBERT PLANK

FEATURING LANCE TAMASHIRO, WILLIE CRAWFORD, JASON PARKER, STU MCLAREN, RAY EDWARDS, DAVID CAVANAGH, ARMAND MORIN & OTHERS

Secret Conversations with Internet Millionaires

"How to Make Money Online with an Internet Marketing Business"

(Featuring Robert Plank, Lance Tamashiro, Willie Crawford, Jason Parker, Stu McLaren, Ray Edwards, David Cavanagh, Armand Morin & Others)

Robert Plank
www.IncomeMachine.com

It's All About You

ATTENTION: You have been granted special access to be a fly on the wall and spy on 10 private conversations with people who have the following in common:

1. Every single person in this book has generated over ONE MILLION DOLLARS in online sales.

2. They didn't inherit the money. Instead, each person built an online business from scratch, from humble beginnings, stumbled at several obstacles, but thanks to an overwhelming desire to meet their goals, they course-corrected their way to success.

3. Whether it was through software, seminars, services, affiliate marketing, or info-products, each person found a way to channel their passion to a side business, remove the 80% that didn't work, and scale up the remaining 20% into a full time income.

4. Each person you'll hear from found a way to move outside their comfort zone -- and use tools like paid advertising, public speaking, list building, social media, or joint venture to generate traffic and put that business on autopilot.

5. All the interviewees listed here are so enthusiastic about their business that they freely share what's working for them -- there's nothing left out, there are no "half baked" action plans, and there are no "closed door" secrets. It's all laid out in the open for you in this guide and it's up to you to apply them.

You might not be a PHP programmer like Robert Plank, a list builder like Lance Tamashiro, a product creator like Kevin Riley, an internet marketer like Willie Crawford, an affiliate marketer like Jason Parker, a business builder like Stu McLaren, a copywriter like Ryan Healy, a strategist like Ray Edwards, a speaker like David Cavanagh, or a teacher like Armand Morin... but you'll apply these techniques in your own business and life.

Your Blog, Membership Site, Email List...
Making Money Online Automatically and...
It's All Done in Under 3 Days

I'll want to get you on the right track to having all this setup within the next 3 days or less:

- Niche & Domain Name
- Blog & Social Proof
- Web Host & Web Page
- Sales Letter & Payment Button
- Email Optin Page
- Membership Site & Drip Content
- Autoresponder Messages
- Traffic

Even in the fancy $2,000... $3,000... even $10,000 courses... teach USELESS skills that are WAY over your head:

- "Now that you have an optin page, I forgot to tell you... you need a blog"
- "Now that you have a blog, I forgot to tell you... you need a sales page"
- "Now that you have a sales page, I forgot to tell you... you need a product"

Sound familiar? Nothing takes you from start to finish... in just one easy weekend, until now:

http://www.IncomeMachine.com

"Time Management" with Robert Plank

About Robert Plank

Robert Plank makes a part-time mid six-figure income on the internet creating information products, software tools, and webinar training.

He has presented over 910 hours of webinar training and has over 1002 pages of sales copy online. He has also published 2,188,669 words worth of reports, transcripts, articles, and membership content in the past 19 months... and has written as many as 100 articles in 1 day.

If you want to build a huge list of responsive email subscribers, create a website that sells automatically, and setup a membership site full of content that excites and engages your visitors, then you need to take Robert Plank's training and use his software tools.

He will show you how to setup a membership site in minutes, demonstrate your system or expertise on a webinar to a live audience, and then drip that content over time to your current and future members, all without any expenses, maintenance or inventory.

Bolaji Oyejide: This is Bolaji Oyejide and today we have the unprecedented opportunity to talk to the inimitable Robert Plank.

Robert is a phenomenal internet marketer. He started making money back in 2003 and his niche back then was PHP programming and establishing a name for himself very early in that phase. He transitioned into making information products with the focus on copywriting and along the way; this person became a webinar crusher. You will be amazed when you hear how many webinars he has done to date. I don't even think I have a current number.

Robert is doing extremely well, making over $40,000 a month from internet marketing. He quit his day job, so we are going to interview him today and jump into Robert's story and start from the beginning. Many of the folks listening to this interview today really want to understand how to get from working a nine to five job and building your internet marketing business on the side to actually making enough and building enough of a structure with your business to fire your day job.

We're also going to get some insight into product creation because Robert is phenomenal at that and we want to know how Robert is able to build such valuable relationships with partners and mentors as well.

Judgment Day: March 25th, 2009

I'm a big fan of yours and I really appreciate the way that you do business. What I'd like to do first is to take people back to March 25 2009. That is a day that will forever live in infamy, if we could borrow some famous words there. Tell us what happened on that day and then could you also give us a hint as to what got you to that point where you could make that break? What does that day mean to you?

Robert: That was the last day of my day job. What happened was I had been marketing online for a number of years and I guess in the few months leading up to it, it had really taken off and it got to the point where I was making $30,000 a year from my day job and I was getting $30,000 a month from my internet stuff so there was a disconnect.

This internet stuff was taking me about two and a half hours a day and I'm making 30 grand every month but then the day job is taking me about nine hours a day, if you include going to and from and lunch break, etc. so it was nine hours a day for a thousand dollars a day. I was making 30,000 a year from the day job and 30,000 a month from online so it was 30 times the difference but even more because of the extra time involved.

That month, I had to quit. I thought I could do both but the day job was more expensive than doing the internet stuff. So I went to see my boss and he had this look on his face... "Oh no what's he want? Is he going to complain about a co-worker, does he want a raise?" I sat there for a second and said, "I'm going to be quitting." And he relaxed and smiled and I haven't looked back.

Bolaji: That's amazing. You got to the point of making $30,000 a month before quitting your day job. I know you started with internet marketing back in 2002 or thereabouts.

It was a seven or eight year journey between when you got started and when you actually quit your job. Could you give us a recap of some of the highlights of that time? For example, I know you were doing a lot of PHP programming to start with and you had quite a bit of success there but you transitioned to information products.

Robert: Yes, I used PHP programming to pay for college. I started out as a freelancer and I would go to marketers because they seemed to have the most money. They would come to me with an idea and I would figure out how much time it would take me, I would give them a quote, which they accepted and then I'd make it. Then I would give them the first draft or the first version of the software product and then they would ask, "Can you add this feature, can you add that feature, can you add this other feature?" So it got to the point where it was really aggravating.

I'm happy I was making $600 a week and $1,000 a week but then the profit would shrink because the next week I spent doing extra stuff that was not agreed on. That led to making a couple of reports, a couple of e-books about what I did. Here are some quick things that you can add to your sales letters to make them convert better by plugging in personalization scripts, quiz scripts, and pop-ups. There were many little things in the report and it would be about 50 to 100 pages and would contain between 7 to 17 PHP scripts that would include the code itself, the instructions, the steps I took to make it and later on videos.

Thousands of Dollars from 7 Days of Part Time Effort

For me it was a lot more fun than doing those big projects because I didn't have a boss. I would look around to find out what people needed, what kind of scripts were they asking for and what other people were charging $100 or $200 for, that I could make in 10 minutes. I made these simple scripts and I presented it to other people as; you could buy all 17 of these different PHP scripts separately and it would cost you $100 each or for $30, you get the 17 scripts plus the documentation on making them with the videos.

I started making products and launching them on the Warrior Forum and on Warrior Special Offers. We didn't think to make it the acronym WSO back then, because everyone called them Warrior Special Offers and it was free to post to WSO. I would post them and I would get a nice launch, at first it was a few hundred dollars when I created one of these products, then it became a few thousand dollars.

At first it took about a month to make these products because I was going to college, and doing freelancing on the side and then I got it down to about seven days, and finally down to about two or three days. It was two or three days of work to make these PHP scripts, make a sales letter, launch it on the Forum for a couple of thousand dollars. Not too bad, right?

Bolaji: That is not too shabby. I recall from reading your story that you ended up making more and more of these information products but at a certain point, either you or somebody observed that perhaps you were putting out too many cheap products. How did you transition mentally into being comfortable charging more for your stuff?

Robert: I received some very good advice from Armand Morin. He had a seminar and his seminar was actually one of the reasons why I quit. It's one of those things were I had a list of pros and cons. On one side I listed all these reasons keeping me employed like a steady pay check, health insurance, socializing and on the other side were reasons to quit and one of those big reasons was that I couldn't really travel.

Any time I wanted to attend a seminar, I had to use my vacation days, but there are only so many vacation days a year. So one of the things that pushed me was not only the income but there was an Armand Morin seminar coming up that I wanted to go to. I've followed him for years, he used software the same as I did and I had to meet this person.

I attended his seminar and during one of the breaks, I decided to check out some different speakers. During the break, Armand had a big crowd of people around talking to him and as I was walking towards the exit and he yells at me... "Robert!"

How to Double Your Sales Instantly

I thought why is Armand Morin talking to me? He said, "I've got something to say to you and if you do this it will double your sales instantly." I asked, "What's your advice?" He said, "You're not going to like this advice, but... double your prices." The next week I took my best-selling software Action PopUp, and changed the price from $27 to $47. It sold more copies at the higher price and made me more money. Since then, I've been increasing the price to everything else.

Bolaji: That is completely counter-intuitive.

Robert: Yes, and it's one of those things we always think by going to Target or Wal-Mart or these retail stores where we think if we price something at $5 we're going to double the number of sales than if we'd priced it at $10 but that's not really the case. I know as far as I'm concerned if I see something for sale for $5 or $10, I'm going to think it's not really worth much. I might see the same kind of thing for $100 and think its worth more.

It's like the example if you see a Honda versus a Lexus, it's pretty much the same car but one is a Honda and one is a Lexus so everyone thinks the higher priced one is more valuable.

Bolaji: I want to talk a little bit more about that because with your history and launching products as Warrior Special Offers, those are typically lower priced than the general marketplace would receive. You talk a lot about training your customers and not getting them used to you charging very low prices. How do you balance doing many WSOs with charging higher prices?

Robert: There are two things about that. First of all the WSO is your entry point. I look at it as there are always at least 5,000 people on the Warrior format at the same time and many of those people don't really know who I am. Many people are starting out or they don't have a lot of money to spend so, I'll give them something small, like a three or four hour course for $10 or $20. Once they are on my list and they know they get results from that, they can move on to something else.

The second part of it is; I have a lot of fun launching a product at a low price and increasing it up. I see many people try to go the opposite way and it doesn't really work out. They try to price high and then they'll run a discount. The problem with that is if you launch something at $2,000 and then one day you discount it to $10, you will get a bunch of people saying oh my God you're awesome I couldn't afford it at $2,000. However, what about the people who actually bought at $2,000, they would say if I'd waited, I could have saved all that money.

It's a lot more fun for me to start it at a low price and then announce the price will be increasing, increase it, and what's funny is that you get sales before and after the price increases every time. I'll have something for $50 and then I'll say the price is increasing to $100 this coming Wednesday and I'll get a bunch of sales and the sales always come right before but then even after the price goes up I'll get people buying right after as well every time. It's not that the sales stop as soon as I increase the price.

Bolaji: That's good. There's a term that you use in one of your blog posts where you talked about "forfeiting the race to free" and that phrase really stuck with me because I think newbies in particular, may have an issue with charging fair market rates for their products where you talk about that sticker shock if you start charging people $10 and then all of a sudden you offer them something that's $500.

Robert: Right, I think you have to start wherever you can, but you do lose people when you increase the price and that's just something that happens. I think also that as far as newbies charging a low amount, my personal opinion is that they just don't believe in themselves that much. I know that was the case for me. They think, "I see people charging $100, $200 but they have all these testimonials". They've been doing this for many years, they've all these results, they're promising millions of dollars but I'm only promising a few hundred dollars or I'm only promising that they can get a list of 100 subscribers so they think I should only be charging $1. I think it's a confidence issue.

My way around that for a while was starting the price low and increasing the price. I was the first person on the Warrior Forum to run dime sales. What happened was that as a programmer I would be trying all kinds of goofy stuff. There is a marketer from way back, named Ken Evoy and he had a product called, "Make Your Price Sell." He had something on the sales letter explaining that the price would slowly drop by a fraction of a penny every second, but if someone bought, the price would increase by a dollar. Have you seen that? I think he took it down a while ago.

Bolaji: I haven't seen that. When I saw the book, it was free.

Robert: The book cost $200 and he was trying to make it behave similar to the stock market where people buy shares in Apple and once Apple goes up, they sell their shares and then Apple goes down. Along the same lines, John Delavera did something similar where every hour the price would go up by a penny or something like that. I used my programming stuff to combine those two ideas and make it where the price would increase per sale.

I would have a whole PHP course with videos, the product, the scripts and the reports. I would say, "The price starts at five cents." Then it was five cents for the first buyer but after they buy, the price would increase for everyone to 10 cents. After they buy, the price for everyone is 15 cents. Then what happens especially on the Warrior Forum where people are going look for a bargain, the price would just blow up. By the time it hit $10 it would slow down, by the time it hit $20 it would slow down even more and it would usually stop around $25 or $30, but the way the math always worked out was the average sale price would be about half of the final price. So if the price stopped at $30 and I got a couple of hundred sales that was the equivalent of a couple of hundred sales at $15.

Bolaji: That is interesting.

Robert: I would get a good payday upfront but what was also very valuable was the list of buyers.

Bolaji: Yes.

Robert: I collected all the email addresses of people who bought from me. It's one thing to have someone get something for free but if someone pays you money for it that means they know how to buy so; they'll know how to buy your next product. They own a credit card, they're willing to pay online and they trust you enough to give you that information.

Then I got crazy and started doing things where every time the price went up, I would edit the title of the post. Back then, when you edited the post it would actually bump it up to the top, this is for bumping a WSO.

Every single sale it would cost $8.32, $8.36 and that pissed a couple of people off and people got really pissed off too if I launched the product at night. They said, the price was $1 six hours ago and now its $10 and that's not fair. It trained people to buy right away.

Bolaji: I see.

Robert: I'm not sure if that was a good thing. I guess it got them used to buying from me but some people would buy without knowing what they were buying because they wanted to get in before it was a couple of dollars more. It was great to have that buyer because every time I launched a product like that, I could get a bunch more sales.

I started experimenting with having a capped number of slots. I was also the first person on the Warrior Forum to do that where I would sell 50 copies at $10 and then I'm shutting it down. Then tomorrow I'll open it up with 50 more copies selling at $20 and that probably got even more people angry. I got the best response by having a set number of slots at a certain price, close it down, and opening it back up at a higher price. Many people wondered... why would I do that and what's your reasoning, it's not like there are a limited number of e-books. The answer is because I can and because when I do, it makes more sales.

Bolaji: I want to talk about scarcity. You've talked a lot about scarcity in your teaching and you practice it not just with price scarcity as you've illustrated very well, but you also do blog scarcity, blog comment scarcity, and webinar replay scarcity. You practice scarcity in several parts of your business and I suppose you do that ultimately because it works. If I could market without scarcity, I would but it works so well.

We've all seen where people do it wrong. They say the price is going to increase at midnight and the next thing is they don't increase the price or they say the price is going to go up to $30 after I sell three more copies. There is a way to fake it, which I don't recommend, but actually saying there were a set number of copies or I'm going to increase the price and then actually doing it, it has a real magical effect. I try that wherever I can and it always happens where I'll have a product or I'll have a membership site and it's just not selling and I'll put a cap on it and then suddenly everyone wants in.

How to Get Hundreds of People to Respond to Everything You Write

I looked at it the same way when I set up a blog. I was active on the Warrior Forum, making about 10 posts a day, and it was frustrating because I would have awesome replies. I would have a lot of stuff to say and I would get maybe 10 or 20 responses, but then the next week the post would be buried on page 25.

Then I realized that I need to make my own website and make a blog, but then I looked at most blogs and most blogs get zero comments. I didn't want to have to choose. Either I post to get many comments and then I'm forgotten about or I have to build my own site and...

Bolaji: You get no comments.

Robert: Yes, and no-one cares. When I did with my first post, I said something like I'm going to post about this and if I get 10 comments I'll make another post. If not, then no big deal, this is will be the only post on this blog.

Another thing that helped was actually taking the list I had built from buyers of my low-ticket sales and sending them my blog. Many people will post something, no one will even know about it, and they won't have scarcity. Scarcity was at first if I get 10 comments, I'll keep posting and some people reacted to that and got angry but it was only a small percentage and the rest of them got it. You're only going to blog if there's a demand for it.

That worked and I started to experiment with those things and after I get 10 comments, I'll close up comments. That way if I blog post and send an email then either you can comment today or you will never have a chance to and that was the other way where I got a lot of people who had never commented on my blog and never commented on anyone's blog who would comment then they got kind of angry. One person told me at a seminar that he didn't even want to comment on my blog but when he saw, there were only five comments left he felt he had to.

I think that anyone who is getting started if they're making a product, they should sell just a certain number of copies and if you sell out there's nothing wrong with that. You can close it down for a while or open it back up maybe at a higher price and with more bonuses.

The same thing with the blog posts. If I get a blog comment on a blog post that's a year or two old, I get annoyed because everyone else is done talking about that. If anyone out there is having trouble getting blog comments, then cap the number of comments. I've a plugin for that called the Action Plugin but you don't even need a plugin once you get your 10 comments edit the post and then turn off comments.

Even something like getting 10 comments is easy because even if you can't get 10 comments, can you get five? Can you get five friends to comment? If you can, reply to each of those comments so it's five comments from other people and five responses from you and that's 10 comments total.

Bolaji: That's crazy. You have a very strange brain but I like how it works.

Robert: I get bored a lot so I try to experiment.

Make Your Words Sell

Bolaji: I want to talk a little bit about products now because you have become a very prolific product creator. Look at your stable of products; I think I found at least 40 information products. This isn't even counting the live webinars; this is just information products that people can buy. You have membership sites, stuff on list building, WordPress plugins, stuff on product creation, and a myriad of other topics. How did you get to the point where you could create so many products in such a small amount of time?

Robert: I got to the point where I was desperate to make a living from making products. We talked earlier about how I was doing freelancing, creating products and doing a day job. You'll never really get rich just from freelancing unless you get lucky. The only way you can get rich from freelancing is by charging a lot per hour but then if you lose clients, you're screwed. You're also screwed if you don't want to work on that day or that week or that month. It got to the point where I wanted to make more money from doing products.

Another thing that I think helped is if you hang out on forums, because you'll see many ideas. What I started noticing was I would post an idea for a product on the forum and then a week later there would be five of them exactly like I had laid out.

I realized that was happening and even if I kept quiet about it and made a product, I would still have some knock-offs. When you're on a public place like a forum, many people post but even more of them are look and watching.

The average person has an idea, and then posts on a forum. They spend all their time making it beautiful, making it perfect and there's people out there taking notes. They find a ghostwriter to write the book or find a programmer to make the products.

I made many of these products because I didn't want to be working free. I didn't want to write down my idea for a script or for a report and then see someone else make it. I want to be the person that made it. I think it's tempting to tell everyone about your idea and feel as if you've accomplished something, and then take a break for six months. It's a lot more profitable to keep quiet about it and make it as fast as possible and put it out there.

This might be just me but after three or four days, or after that first week then I'm going to get bored with the idea. As soon as I have a good idea, I make the simplest version and put it out there. On more than one occasion even when I had the day job, I would get an idea at nine or 10 o'clock at night and I would stay up all night making the PHP script, debugging it, making the manual, making the sales letter, mailing it out at six in the morning then go to work. I would check back during the lunch break to see how things played out. I knew if I didn't jump on it right away, a million things would probably go wrong. Someone would steal the idea, get to it before me, I'd get bored, or it would be half finished. I don't really trust myself to stick with an idea for too long. I need to put it out there as fast as possible and get it selling on its own.

Keep it Shippable, Stupid

Bolaji: I want to talk a little bit about a concept typically called "Keep It Simple Stupid," but you call it "Keep It Shippable Stupid" and making the point about keeping it shippable, you suggest we reject the pressure to build out the entire sales funnel upfront. Instead of having the free article followed by the solo email ad, the affiliate program, the squeeze page, the pre-sales email, the sales letter, the checkout page, the upsell page, and the download page, keep it as simple as having your sales letter, your check out page and the product that you're going to send. Is that an approach that helps you get these things out of the door quickly?

Robert: Yes. For me, I'll get excited about something to a point but I'll get a lot more excited about it if I get money. I see it all the time. They'll have an idea for a product and they'll get the domain name for it, they'll get the perfect graphics made, they'll make the pre-launch videos, the upsell, the down sell but they won't even make their product. You've already put weeks of effort into this, you didn't make the product, you didn't make any money for it yet so I'd rather put it out there as simple as possible and make some money upfront and then build it.

I think what hurts a person is the information now that's it's all developed it's too accessible. What I mean is... back in the day an upsell page was news to us. Most of us didn't know about an upsell page.

I went to the first Warrior event and the big takeaway I got from that event was that you could have more than one upsell. It had never crossed my mind to have a $20 product, upsell a $300 product, upsell a $200 product, I was thinking one upsell, and that's it. During the whole three-day event, I learned all kinds of stuff, but the biggest piece of advice was having more than one upsell.

There are people now that might learn that their first day or their first week and think they need to have all these pieces in place when they're just extra. A lot of us were selling for years without a membership site, without even a very good sales letter, without an upsell, without a list or a follow up sequence. All of that stuff can come later. You see these launches happen and you see it in a different order. You see the pre-launch videos and the emails pretty much first but that's not necessarily the order you should make them.

The other thing that people forget is that I've seen some launches even from some big name marketers where they would say we're launching on June 1st but as they get closer they say we're going to have to change the launch date to June 30th and I'll think "what happened?". Well what happened was they did it in the wrong order. They spent all their time on the promotion not on the product and so they had to adjust up. If you hope for the best and plan for the worst then make something that you could sell today. Maybe it's not the best, even if it's only a 20-page report, even if its software that only does some of the functionality, can it stand on its own. Is it worth the price you're charging and does it work? I would rather have a piece of software that's simple and works than something that is advanced and doesn't work.

Daily Video Challenge

Bolaji: I wonder if you could talk a little bit about a challenge that you entered into with one of your buddies, Jason Fladlien, in late 2008 before you quit your day job,. From what I read, you both entered a challenge to create a certain number of quality videos each week for 55 weeks. That's a huge commitment, what in the world were you persons thinking and how did the challenge go?

Robert: I think it was to make a video every day for 30 days and then to make 50 of them in one day. The way I look at it is once you do 50 videos in a day then making 10 or 20 in a day is not a big deal. I wanted to see how far I could push it. You see people repeatedly start posting videos on YouTube or they'll make a blog and they'll be excited about it for a week or for a day or two and then they'll be done. They'll write five posts a day for a couple of days and then will be done.

I think if you can do something every day for a month, then suddenly it will feel weird if you don't do it. As an example, if you went swimming every day for a month or went running every day for a month, then on day 31, you didn't go swimming or you didn't go running then you would feel somewhat weird. I wanted to do more video because video is so cheap to do now and so easy. You can take out your iPhone, hit a button, talk, and then upload to YouTube right on the phone.

Back then when Flip cameras first came out and it was a similar thing. Hit one button, record it and now you can put it on YouTube. YouTube at the time was the number two search engine, so I really wanted to have a lot of videos on YouTube but I didn't want to fall in that trap of making a bunch of videos on one day and then nothing the rest of the month.

I guess what that came to was first announcing it in public so that if I messed up it would be less embarrassing for all those people. I had a certain amount of pain and pleasure motivating me and I had to make sure that the pain of not doing it was worse than the pain of doing it and the pleasure of doing it was better than the pleasure of not doing it, if that makes sense. I said to my subscribers if you want to do this with me then you can as well. I didn't ask them to do it because I know there's only a small percentage who will actually do stuff if you ask them to but I know that some people did it every day out of the month and some people did it for half the month.

I don't recommend that people do that for every single thing they do, but it helps every now and then to light a fire under your butt and say here's my goal for the month and I'm going to update you every day of the month to make sure I'm on track and you can do it too. That always makes the best blog posts and the best products when you're sharing what you do instead of trying to invent stuff.

I did that with the videos and I think even before I did that to get my first $25,000 a month and my first $30,000 a month and it was the same kind of thing. I would tell my subscribers this month I want to make $25,000. I think at the time I was averaging about 10, so this is going to be a huge jump.

Bolaji: That is a big jump.

Robert: I was pretty sure I could do it and I told my subscriber lists at the beginning I'm going to be launching one resale rights product per week, one new product per week and an old product for a week. I want you to be on the lookout for lots of emails from me because I'll be updating you every day with my total. What I ended up telling them was what I had made up to that point and what I had left to reach my goal. I've got 26 days left which means that I need to make this amount today, every day onward, and both those times the $25,000 came up and the $30,000 came up. I hit those goals because it would have been so embarrassing to miss.

Bolaji: That's true.

Robert: And I was taking consistent action every day.

Bolaji: I think one of the most popular posts on your blog has to do with you asking your subscribers what they think your most hated word is, at least within the context of business, and the guesses were all over the map. A few people actually got it right. The word that you had in mind, the four-letter word that you hate the most, is the word "work."

You went on to elaborate how too many people have a negative connotation about work but if you can actually make the stuff that you have to do fun, make it a challenge, turn it into a game, it actually goes a lot more quickly. It sounds like you have been doing that quite a bit in your business.

Robert: Yes. If you look at anyone who has made it real big, what happens first is you have to put in a lot of hours and a lot of work but the thing they all have in common versus people who don't make it is that the people who've made it really enjoyed what they did. They had an overwhelming desire to make it happen, they had a lot of passion and they have been putting in 12-hour days, but to them it was having fun. They would have done those 12 hours free.

I don't know if you notice but you'll keep using the same words repeatedly or you'll hear people use the same words repeatedly, do you know Mark Joyner?

Bolaji: Yes.

Robert: Years and years ago, he had a policy in his office with his employees that they couldn't use the word 'wait'. This was because people would say things like I'm waiting for this to happen, I'm waiting on this person and he kept hearing this word so much that it drove him crazy and he said you couldn't use the word "wait." You can use a word to replace the word 'wait' and what's going to happen is you'll almost say the word "wait," stop yourself and readjust and you'll feel like something is wrong but eventually you'll change your thinking.

That's very powerful if you notice a word or something that you always say. People always say we're in such a down economy, then someone else says it, and even if it's not true at first then it becomes true because everyone believes it. What happened with me was I found myself using the word 'work' a lot; I've got to go to work, I've got to work on this and then I would hear that a lot from my subscribers. If they sold software, they would say things like help me get your software to work or my software doesn't work and I would say the same thing. I heard this word so much it drove me crazy.

We have to stop using that word "work." I didn't use the word at all for a couple years. Now I use it a little bit but I was using it too much. If you go on the Warrior Forum, you'll see certain phrases repeated repeatedly. If you talk to your subscribers, certain phrases will be repeated over and over.

As an example of that, you mentioned Webinar Crusher at the beginning of this call. That course teaches people how to run their own webinars and I would ask people what stops you from running a webinar and the answer repeatedly was the phrase "prep time." They didn't say "the amount of time to get it ready" or "preparation" or even "preparation time," they all used this exact phrase "prep time" over and over and over.

Recently when I was launching a course called Product University that was priced at over $2,000, I got many responses from people saying, "Robert, you shouldn't be pricing this high, you're out of touch."

Even those people who couldn't afford $10 were saying "out of touch". If I were them that's a phrase I wouldn't use, but that's also something I started using in my marketing so it works both ways. Either a word brings you down or pulls you back up. If you're the kind, of person that has subscribers who always say things to you like "this is out of touch", then maybe if you hit on that and you say, "If you think this is out of touch then there's this". I sent an email that said something like if your friends and your family say you're out of touch for believing you can make a product, then you should adjust your thinking in this certain way.

If there are words that you use like "work" or "angry" or "enraged", try going for 30 days without using that word or if you use that word keep a note of that and don't say it next time. The Eskimos have hundreds of words for "ice" because they use ice all the time. There are certain tribes out in the jungle that don't have a word for war and they've been at peace for hundreds of years because they can't even think what war is because they don't have a word to associate with it.

Bolaji: That's very interesting. It's fascinating how you started out as a PHP programmer, you picked up copywriting skills and started to teach but somewhere along the way I guess you had so many efficient ways of getting things done that you really started to teach a lot about productivity and we're hearing some of your philosophies in that area.

One that I would like to touch on is this issue of marketers dealing with losses or "failure", that's one thing that is prevalent when you're working for yourself, you're going to fail a lot and it can be very discouraging for the newbies in particular who are out there. How have you dealt with failures or losses and how do you motivate yourself to move forward just by falling down?

Robert: I've seen people do a launch and they won't make a lot of money, but in internet marketing, you can make something really quickly. I think if people have a failure they should really count themselves lucky because it's not as if they had to spend five years making a physical product or they had to buy an office building to do real estate.

With internet marketing, you can have an idea right now, get a domain, make a product, get the sales letter and it's on there. If you launch something and it fails you can go ahead and make another product and I think that if it takes you six months or a year to make a product or make a report then yes failing is going to be rough so that's why you have to do it as quickly as possible. Do it in a few days, do it in a week so that if it fails then you readjust or make a new one.

Why People Fail

As far as people making a product and failing, there are a few common reasons for that. One reason is that no one wants the product and that's why you need to keep a pulse on your subscribers, go to forums, not necessarily to talk but to see what your competition is selling, what is everyone talking about, what's the problem?

Going into a niche with no competitors is not a good thing. You don't necessarily want to copy but if someone has a WordPress blog or someone has a piece of software or a report that is a really hot seller and you think you can do a lot better, then go ahead and model that. One reason why a product might not sell is it's something no one wants or a certain crowd won't go for it. If your crowd is in the Warrior Forum, check and see what the Warriors are talking about then make a product about that and make small products.

One of my biggest jumps in income was from making my first WordPress products. I had been teaching PHP programming and here and there and people on the Warrior Forum were talking about WordPress. Blogging was starting to take off as far as internet marketers doing it. There were not that many products about it and I put it out there thinking I only put one week into this, people on the Warrior Forum are talking about WordPress, and there aren't that many paid products about WordPress. I think it ended up making $8,000 in sales that week and then the next week I sold the resale rights to it for another $8,000.

I was surprised at the time. WordPress was not a real big thing as far as internet marketers so I was really nervous but I had this attitude of either it will sell or it won't and if it doesn't I'm only out a couple of days versus a few years. That's another reason to have a small product.

Then as far as if there are no sales at all, the problem is either that the offer sucks, it isn't right or that not enough people are seeing it. If the offer sucks, it might be the wrong topic, a weird price or it might be priced too high or too low. I've had classes where I've priced too high. I had a product about how to do blogging, I priced it at a couple of hundred dollars, and no one went for it.

Then I put out a version of it for $20. It was just a report and everyone bought it and loved it. There are some topics that you can't price and the perceived value will never break through. There are WordPress themes for $200, and $300 but you won't see many WordPress plugins for that price unless they're membership software. You certainly don't see WordPress plugins for $500 or $1,000; no one is going to believe a price that high is worth it.

On the other hand, if you see a real estate course for $10 saying flip your house for no money down and get $20,000, that's not very believable. The offer might not be right and that's all the more reason to look at what's selling right now and look to see if everyone is selling this product for $100, then I'll price around $100. It's cool to be creative but it pays a lot more to not copy, but model what others are doing right and that way you are doing something that's proven.

Another issue we discussed is the list. A big reason why the WSOs and the Warrior forums helped me is that it helped me build a list. If you only have a list of 100 people and you email them an offer and you get two or three sales... that's great. You see people who only have a list of 100 people and get two or three sales and feel sad about it. No, you've converted at 3%... you're awesome; you just need to build a bigger list.

You need to have all the components. Not only have products but build a list of subscribers as well.

Bolaji: There's one challenge that strikes me with building a successful online business. We alluded to this earlier. When you look at a complete online business, there are several pieces to it. You want to have your offer, have traffic, have an upsell product or upsell funnel, also a thriving auto responder series for your list. Often internet marketers really struggle to focus. What's the best way for dealing with information overload and a lack of focus?

Robert: I think an easy thing to do is put a freeze on your buying habits for this month. I've seen people who every day open up their laptop and the start page is the Warrior Forum and they say, "What am I going to buy today?" They would rather buy 10 products for $10 than one for $100 and that means they're only going to devote two or three days to one product, which isn't enough time for them to implement it. They'll buy the second product two days later and I guess the idea is one out of 10 will work, but I think that maybe one out of one will work.

I think you should stop buying stuff and look at what you have. I think I pulled my list once and 95% of them had at least one resale rights product that they had not put to use, it was sitting on the hard drive. Most people already have something to put online and have some kind of course they just haven't gone through yet. It might be my personality but if there's too much clutter on my desk or on my hard drive or in my house, I get really pissed off and get in a negative state. If I buy a course and I haven't finished it, I feel bad, so whatever you've already bought, go through it. Try not buying anything else for a month, except for my stuff of course and your stuff, but don't buy anything else for the rest of the month and put what you have to use.

Retrain Yourself to Focus

We talked earlier about retraining your subscribers, but you also have to retrain yourself. It's a bad habit to buy new stuff and have five different projects going. I used to be like that; I would have five projects going at the same time and then only one or two of them would be done. You have to have discipline, some kind of self-control. If you have five different ideas you're not going to work on all five, you're only going to work on one right now.

Then have those other ideas in mind for when the first product is online, the sales letter is done, the button's done, I make my first 10 sales, then I'll work on the next one. I don't like people to have to do a list but I do think you should be working on one thing at a time. Even if you have five things or twenty things in mind, you know there's the one that you know is going to make you the most money, has the best chance of working or you can finish fastest. Work on one thing at a time.

Bolaji: Yes, that is really useful information and I've suffered from some of those challenges in terms of lack of focus in my business over the years, probably most of us have. In your particular business, I think some of your success in being able to focus so well and churn out so many products in short amounts of time might be due to your inherent personality but you've also built structures around yourself and surrounded yourself with support people that really enhance your ability to focus. Like the challenge, you did with Jason, I know that you work with one of your partners, Lance Tamashiro; you people do a lot of stuff to give each other accountability. Could you talk a little bit about the benefit of surrounding oneself with people who can give you accountability and help you to stay on the straight and narrow path?

Robert: All right. That comes down to it's easy to let yourself down but it's really tough to let someone else down. If you don't show up somewhere, you let your wife down, you let your kids down, and that's much more powerful than letting yourself down. I played on that. I worked with a man named Steven Schwartzman. He was a copywriter and I needed to be more stuck in. We all have those plateaus where our income stays the same, we don't put out enough products or we don't do enough marketing and Steven and I had a couple of products together.

I wouldn't really call him my business partner because we weren't doing everything together like Lance and I are right now. This was while I still had my day job, I would call him and tell him that I have four things I have to do and every day it was four things. I've tried different ways of doing it but its always four things. I have to write this chapter of my book, send out this email to my list, make these five posts on the Warrior Forum and I have to spend 10 minutes writing articles.

At the beginning of the day I would tell him my four things and he would tell me his four things then at the end of the day I would call him back and tell him what I had and hadn't gotten done and he would do the same thing with me. I was still working my day job and sometimes didn't have time to do them before, after, and during my breaks.

If you didn't email your list because you bought a WSO, you would feel bad because you're letting someone else down. You promised to do something and then you ended up not doing it. I did that with Steven and then when I worked with Jason we started doing that by email. When I started working with Lance we had something even cooler, we set up a private membership site for us because the emails became too much to deal with. Also every time management guide these days tells you not to check your email because it's so tempting to get distracted or there's the

WSO of the day or Frank Kern launched something brand new so there are all these distractions.

The Biggest Productivity Secret of All: Four Daily Tasks

I needed a way to stay on track, do my four tasks, and not necessarily check email that day or at least not first thing in the morning. We set up a membership site where we were the only two people who could log in and every day I would make a new post. I would type up my four things, publish it and he could see it. He would publish his own post and then at the end of the day I would leave a comment underneath those tasks and say that I finished number one, three, and four, but didn't finish number two.

That became our accountability site and we have a record of everything I've done and I could see what wasn't done because that's the real danger of having an accountability partner or having the four tasks. Let's use the article writing. You might do three things but that fourth item, writing articles, you were going to do on Monday, you move to Tuesday. On Tuesday, you have more four things and your fourth item is articles again.

By having it all on one site you can notice that by Thursday it's been four days in a row where I said I would write articles and I didn't, so on Friday I need to do the articles first or maybe the articles aren't that important and I shouldn't keep them on my list. That's really helpful as far as seeing where you are going, where you are wasting time and what's really important.

Bolaji: Wow, that is simple but it seems very effective.

Robert: It is. I see people who try to get fancy, they try to make it 5 daily tasks or 20 daily tasks but it gets back to that whole thirty-day challenge we talked about before. I was there too. I would do 20 things in one day but then would take the rest of the week off because I was so tired.

If you complete four things every day, it's a consistent action. Even on weekends I will do four daily tasks which means on Saturday it might be half an hour of work for all four, but on a weekday it might be three or four hours of work for all four. A task for any particular day might be as big as writing five articles or making a three-minute video. It depends on how busy of a day it is but that guarantees that you will do four things a day and whatever that is times 365 days, results in thousands of things per year.

Bolaji: Awesome. Folks, in respect for Robert's time, I'm going to go ahead and wrap it up. Robert, as we close I'd love to know what your 2011 business goals are and what else we should expect from you this year?

Robert: Something I've been working on a lot this year is doing more recurring income and membership sites. As far as selling a product, you can either charge one time, have a fixed term like an installment plan, a payment plan where someone pays you five payments monthly or you can have a continuity site, a site where somebody pays you for ever and ever. That's the nut I'm trying to crack this year because it's the hardest sale of all.

I can do a pretty good job selling the payment plan, but selling someone on the idea that you're going to join this site and pay forever and ever, month after month, that's really tough. I've been doing it but it comes back to price training. My goal for this month is to get people on a month after month recurring payment plan.

Bolaji: Awesome. We know you blog at robertplank.com but are there any other websites that you'd like to share with the audience today?

Robert: Sure. One site that I think everyone should go to and take this training is called membershipcube.com because everyone needs to have a membership site. Even the accountability site I just mentioned that only Lance and I had access to was a membership site.

We use WishList Member on that and if I go to a seminar or listen to someone's course, I take notes and post it there. No one else can see it, but it's a place where I can go back to all my stuff. I post my split tests results and my swipe files there. It also uses membership software to hold my downloads because whether you are launching a WSO or a $2,000 course, it helps me to have everything in a membership site that I can get back to at any time.

If someone loses their download link, they can use the lost password button and get it back. If you want to update your software, add bonuses, enable people to comment, add a forum, have a community, or put in fancy upsells, it's a lot easier and it makes you a lot more money if you put it inside of a membership site.

The software I use that I think everyone should use is not my software, it's called WishList Member and it costs $300 and you can use it as many times as you want, but if you're on Membership Cube I will buy that for you. I will go to the creators and get a license in your name. Not only will I show you my membership sites, and show you how to set up the software but I will give you the software and will give you many of my plugins that I use to do cool things such as drip out the contents.

If you have a product and you want to cut your report or video course into pieces and you want to charge $100 but can get people to pay $10 a month to get the course, then you install some plugins, go to this screen, click that link and I will show you everything. There is a whole community inside there of other membership site owners.

There are challenges that will keep you accountable, motivated, on track to launching your membership site, which includes setting it up, getting the sales letter going, getting the content made, and building the email list, all of this is inside membershipcube.com.

"Starting Your Own Business" with Lance Tamashiro

About Lance Tamashiro

Before hearing about internet marketing, I was an IT computer nerd for most of the 2000's. In Las Vegas and Salt Lake City, I worked as a "Database Administrator" which is the nerdiest of the nerd programming types.

During that time, I got married and had a daughter. One day, while sitting in my office, I realized things needed to change. I looked around the internet and discovered people were making money online, actually helping other people, and bringing value to the lives of others. I tried every "push button technique" that doesn't work: I created a blog, added AdSense, and flipped websites.

I found a mentor who told me I needed to build a list, so I built a list of 6000 subscribers in two months. Then I realized that "cut and paste" affiliate marketing did not generate enough income. Therefore, I created and marketed products about how I built my list, how I automated sales, and used myself as a case study the entire way.

If you too want to succeed, then you should apply those exact strategies in your own business. Additionally, you need a mastermind or partner that understands your excitement when you make progress, has members with different skill sets to learn from, and help you to make consistent progress.

My business partner Robert Plank and I now operate a million dollar business where we market training courses (Membership Cube, Webinar Crusher, and Double Agent Marketing) and sell software (WordPress Drip, Webinar Optin, and Backup Creator).

Fleeing Corporate America

Lance: I'm not a marketing type; I have never done anything with marketing in my life up until getting involved with this internet-marketing thing. My background is actually from corporate America, I was an official IT computer nerd for a little more than a decade. I worked on databases, which is the nerdiest of the nerd programming types.

I was a total DBA type and one day, I'm sitting in the office and I'm just listening to people telling me all the things, these ridiculous things to do while I'm pretending I'm busy. How we all do with our day jobs, and thinking all this stuff you're telling me is ridiculous, I'm not going to do any of it anyway, can you leave so I can get back to the internet, look at the news.

I was if I have to spend five more years here I'm going to kill myself. There's nothing worse to me than going to the office and sitting there, pretending you're doing something productive, to make your boss happy and being told to do things that are ridiculous tasks anyway. So I started look around the internet, found the Warrior forum, found all of these other places, found out people were making money online, actually helping other people and bringing value to other people's lives and just started getting involved in it.

I goofed around for a year. I did all the stuff that doesn't work, the push button stuff, making a blog, do ad sense, do all this stuff that really doesn't work. Then in July of 2008, I hooked up with a person named Jason Parker who's a good Warrior and he tells me to build a list.

I decided I was going to build a list. In summer 2008, I hooked up with him and started building a list. I built a list of about 5,000 or 6,000 in a couple of months and then figured out that I needed a product. There's many good ways of doing affiliate marketing but the way I was doing it was all wrong. It wasn't providing any value to anybody, I was cutting and pasting emails every day and just sending spam out to people. Then I met a person named Robert Plank and he said "dude you've got this huge list, figure out how to start making products" and so I started creating products about how I built my list and used myself as a case study.

Jason: Now I don't know if you and Robert had a chance to speak about this but I actually interviewed Robert recently and he told me an interesting story that he hated your guts at first?

Lance: I was a student of his; I was taking $300 to $500 courses every single month from him. He would get on the call and say "I don't care what Lance did, I hate him, get off the call". I'm like dude I'm paying you money.

The weird thing is though it really motivated me to prove to him that I could implement his systems and I made it my goal, I was making about $3,000 a month at the time, so I wasn't making that much money. I told my wife I'm going to put this huge amount of money into this new coaching program Robert has. She wanted to know why because I already knew all that stuff, and I explained that my whole point was to turn him into my business partner from this class. I knew how his classes were structured, so I went in to be the best student there was. I did all of his accountability stuff and finally I cracked him and the rest is history.

Jason: Well you know, he told me a story about inviting you to some conference and saying it was OKAY to attend and not pay.

Lance: Yes, he's done all sorts of things like that to me. I think the lesson in all of this is, it's a metaphor for building your own business and that really is it. We have so many students and the ones that make it its great because they get that and the ones that don't you see them get right up to the point of success and then they stop, or they start doing something else. When you feel you're at that edge, that point of stopping or that point where there's just too many barriers, you should be really happy because that means you're there.

What Makes Successful People Different...

If building our own business was the easy problems, everybody would be doing it and everybody would be successful. The thing that's going to make everybody different is those who can recognize that you're at one of those moments and rather than jump ship, it's time to really focus and get over it, and you're at those crossroads.

Jason: Absolutely. The one thing that Robert ended his conversation about you by saying, "Lance basically used to ask me all these questions and finally one day he just stopped asking me questions and every time I would tell him to do something and he would do it, and do it to the best of his ability. He just blew me away with his implementation". So many times, people that e-mail me and are on my webinars and calls are too focused on trying to do things perfectly.

You know what, it's never going to be there, just this last week I released a book that I had written and I got it on Amazon, but guess what. If I had never just finally done it and hit submit it would still be on my hard drive. If I had never sat down and said you know what, I'm not that great of a writer but I'm going to give this a shot, it would still be in my head and it wouldn't make any money. It wouldn't get me any of the notoriety that it's been getting me this past week. It's exciting to be able to go to my Mom and hand her a copy of the book.

Lance: Isn't that the best?

Jason: Yes and I didn't tell her I was writing it so we were all hanging out on Sunday and I said," oh by the way check this out". Their jaws hit the ground but guess what, I guarantee you there's something that's wrong in that book, there's probably some typos in there and, I mean I'm not saying don't do a good job on something, you've got to just do it and take action.

Lance: You know the whole perfectionism thing that people think they have to get stuff perfect, you should say make it the highest quality you can, but the perfectionism stopping point is exactly what I was doing, it's just an excuse. At the end of the day, what we're all doing online is info product creation and info product stuff; it's a lot different to sell something that you have actually created versus selling something that your boss told you to sell.

It's about you, it's different and it doesn't matter if it's a blog post, an email, or a book, because it's scary the first time, you do it. That is the point, if you just get it out there, it's exciting, you'll do it again because of that excitement, and that's what so many people don't get to experience. If they would just keep it simple and not over think it, you'll instantly be a success.

People want push button stuff that doesn't work, but then when you actually give them something that simple and say this is what works, do it. Now they want complex and I'm saying, "You bought the push button stuff knowing it doesn't work, you wanted it simple, and I showed you how to do it simply and now you're saying that you want it harder, but you haven't even done what's simple yet. Therefore, what you should do is just launch something because you can always improve it later.

Biggest Mistake: Systemization!

Jason: Absolutely, you know speaking of not being a perfectionist, I'm sure there have been some mistakes that you have made in your career as an internet marketer. What would you say that your biggest mistake was?

Lance: The first mistake that I've ever made with marketing is first not getting a good customer support system in place from the very beginning. I used to pride myself that I could answer every email within five minutes and when you're getting started that's a fun thing to do. The problem is you're setting an unrealistic expectation, usually for customers that aren't paying enough for your customer support. So you're actually losing money, if you're spending time doing hours of customer support on a $97 product. You're either not pricing your product right, your product is not good enough or you're getting the wrong customers.

What I've done now, so things like setting that expectation of how fast you respond, yes it's good to respond quickly but it's also good to set an expectation. We've recently switched all of our stuff to a product called ZenDesk, we pay $9 a month for it, and we run our entire business off it. It's nice because your customer is acknowledged and gets notices as soon as things happen.

Jason: How would that compare, if you were familiar with it, with something like OSTicket?

Lance: We stopped using OSTicket, because it only works on a single site installation. So because we have multiple products and websites, we can't use OSTicket.

Jason: Because you have to log in to a different, install for each product?

Lance: Exactly, with OSTicket you use a single site installation.

Jason: Yes, that's ugly.

Lance: ZenDesk consolidates it all for us; I even think they have a trial you can use. The second mistake I made was not doing enough customer appreciation type stuff. What I mean is people are blown away, especially when you're getting started, to receive acknowledgment from you. If somebody buys from you, when you see that sale come in or the next day, pick up the phone and call them, thank them. Don't sell them anything, just call them and say I saw you bought WP Drip and I wanted to make sure that it went OKAY, that you were able to get it, and install it, just thank them. You'll be amazed at how, you can turn numerous $47, or $17 customers into lifelong multiple thousand dollar customers just by using that one little tactic. And then they know you're a real person and who does that?

Jason: Hardly anyone.

Lance: I would do this, if I was just getting started today with my $7 products. Because chances are, you're going to be able to keep up with that volume as you're getting started and that's how you build a loyal following. To do that I get a Skype number, on Skype for $30 a month or a year you can get a phone number and you can call all over the world. So I don't care where they buy from me, I pick up the phone and call them if I have a number for them.

Scaling Up

Jason: Sweet, yes that is cool. Then I guess, when you get to the level that you persons are at, you could hire someone to make those calls for you. But like you said starting out, you can do them yourself.

Lance: Yes and it's amazing, people will read every email you send them after that. I mean you're now on a completely different level than anybody else is.

Jason: Sure, absolutely. Well you know I was going to ask you, if you started over today how would you do things, I think you actually answered that within that question. You would get a better support system and you would work on developing those customers more by making phone calls.

Lance: Yes and I'd start with a small $7 report and I would use forum marketing, it doesn't matter what niche. I would market to that forum.

Jason: I see, let me ask you a question. Many people consider you and Robert mentors of theirs, I mean I do as being part of the Webinar Crusher class. Who do you consider as a mentor, who do you look to for information?

Lance: The main person that I look up to is Armand Morin. I really respect what he's done and how he's built his business. He's one of the few real multimillion dollar a year gurus online. But he's done it a lot different than some of the other big gurus. You don't see lots of mailing for his products. You don't see the whole group mailing like you do some of the other big gurus and what I really respect about the way he's built his business is he's done it without owing favors like that to other people, you know. He doesn't have to mail people, he can mail people if he wants to but he has built his whole business, and it's self-sufficient where many of the other gurus really need each other to help keep their list fresh and help keep it building.

Jason: Yes, you know, it was actually one of his live events that got me into the internet-marketing world. I also come from a corporate background very much like you and had gone through some rough times. I was into programming things and a friend of mine told me what she did online and I just thought I don't really understand that.

A friend invited me to a conference and I took this friend with me who, in his own right he was a multi-millionaire and I just thought if anybody could see through a line of BS it's my friend. So I'm going to take him and that way if this is like AmWay or something, he'll say "Let's get out of here, this is some kind of weird stuff or whatever". And so we went through half the day and while we were at lunch I looked at my friend and said "So what do you think about this person?" He looked me dead in the eye and said that he was the real deal. "I don't know how he makes all his money but I'm telling you he's telling the truth".

Lance: Yes, he is. I've been to his house, he is telling the truth.

Jason: That was enough for me. I think sometimes it takes that moment of epiphany where you just say wow this is real, I think I can do this and then you start putting the actions in behind it.

Lance: Unfortunately, I think so many people that come online get caught up with the people that aren't real and one of the big things that I would tell anybody is, if you're trying to do any kind of business, whether it's online, offline, AmWay, multi-level marketing, whatever it is, do some quick research. If somebody sends, you an email and they tell you to buy their system because they do a ton a webinars all the time, then take five seconds and type in their name and webinars and see if anything comes up.

If somebody sends you an email and tells you that they know this system for making niche sites in all of these different niches and it really works, then type in their name and a couple of the examples and see if anything's there. Unfortunately, a large percentage of what goes on in this market space is hype and its people trying to mimic and they just don't know any different. So find the people who actually have the results.

Many people think great that means they can't get started, but my first product was about how to build a list of 100 people. My competition was telling people he was going to teach them how to build tens of thousands of people lists. I didn't know how to do that, but what I did know how to do, was build a list of a hundred. So it put me in a unique position because once I taught people how to make a list of 100, I was still growing my list. What do they need to know how to grow next? Well maybe a list of 5,000, and now that I know how to do that, that's my next product. Along the way, I learned different techniques that I was able to teach people.

Jason: That's fantastic. What future goals do you have specifically for your business in the next five years?

Lance: Well as most people may or may not know about us, I only think of my business as my four daily tasks a day. I have numbered goals.

Honestly, especially with running your own business, it's nice to have goals but things change every single day. So I really just try to every single day to pick four things that I'm going to do for my business that I know moves my business in the right direction. I have some general guidelines, but honestly, I don't plan very far ahead. I try to just plan each day as it comes.

"Rapid Product Creation" with Kevin Riley

About Kevin Riley

Kevin Riley is an entrepreneur with over 30 years of experience building and running businesses.

He runs a successful information product business from the comfort of his home office in Osaka, Japan. And now, he shows you how you too can create a successful infopreneur business and live anywhere in the World.

Don't Assume Anything

Kevin Riley: I go systematically when I create something. I like to teach in a very detailed way. I make many screenshots and try not to assume anything. I do assume that the person that's getting one of my guides doesn't know a thing about what they're about to do.

I imagine they just setup their computer, and this is the first thing they found online. I've been told that attitude is really helpful to many people. I only have had a few people not like my guides.

Robert: But it is not who you're targeting, right?

Kevin: Exactly. Yes. I told you it's good.

Robert: I bought three or four of your guides. I think it will pull up many people when they're trying to make information products and they're trying to give people every single choice and trying to be really thorough.

It sounds like your solution to that is instead of really thinking about being thorough or appealing to everyone, you're just appealing to the newbies and putting it to screenshots. It sounds like screenshot is your secret weapon, right?

Kevin: Yes, yes. It's also a secret weapon so you don't have to do as much writing because if you take one of my essays, that are about a hundred page and use screenshots, it boils down to less than 10 pages of a writing.

Kevin: It makes it a little easy. You take screenshots and write simple directions in between.

Robert: I wish they let us write that way back in school.

Kevin: Yes, yes. University term papers? I knew you would get that.

Robert: Yes. I remember now. I think I bought a product teaching me what to do after a product launch.

You went as far as saying that it was like you put out a new product, launch it, and then you get affiliates. You went as far as saying, "Eventually, maybe you can run your own offline seminar." And "You know what, go to Yahoo Maps and take a screenshot of the directions from the airport to the seminar."

Kevin: Yes. I forgot I did that, but yes, that's the kind of stuff I like to do. Why make it difficult for people?

I do that offline, too. For example, if I want to go in a local restaurant and I'm looking it up online, I think they should have a map to their place because I can't really tell where your restaurant is. If you give me a good map, I could get there and you're going to have a customer. It's as simple as that, right?

Robert: It didn't even cross their mind.

Kevin: Exactly.

Robert: They just think, "I've got this online. How come no one's showing up?" Just like I see so many people say, "I made a blog. How come I don't have a million comments yet?" Because they haven't done the right steps. You like these really short, simple, step-by-step guides. How did you start doing that?

Kevin: I started with these guides in the internet-marketing niche in 2006. At that time, I was actually writing a guide to natural health, naturally lowering your blood pressure, which still sells to this day.

I've been in the offline business for years with all kinds of things. People kept asking, "Hey, Kevin, we are seeing all these conversations, could you give us some of your ideas?" I thought, "Why don't I create products for these persons there's a lot of questions to be answered here," and that's how it started.

Simple & Short How-To Guides

I started creating guides that showed different things. One of my early ones on sales is how to put together an information product. Just a small guide like the ones that I do. I was successful doing a lot of that and sold that for years until finally I thought I have the gates and I'm pulling off the market.

Robert: You just update it, and add newer screen shots.

Kevin: I created a couple of new ones and made it better with updated screenshots.

Robert: All right.

Kevin: The new versions are better. I always push to get better and better. I think that's something you have been crazy with your products and stuff, and putting out your approach.

Robert: Yes. That's all you can do. When I look at my old membership sites or reports, I'm thinking, "Really?" I cringe at some of my old sales letters. But they made sales and you are always improving.

Kevin: Yes. We always look and cringe at our letters. I cringed at that first report and thought, this is not that great, but people were saying, "Wow, It's fantastic. We love it." And I'm thinking, "Really?"

Robert: That's all that matters that they bought it and they loved it. Who cares what you think? What THEY think is more important.

Kevin: Yes. In a way, it actually goes to show that you have to keep it simple and people will like it.

Robert: You mentioned a couple of really interesting things that I want to make sure everyone listening understands. First of all, you were on a message board and a foreman. You kept getting pulled into these conversations. It's kind of like the formula for starting out and for getting advice and giving advice.

I don't know about you, but eventually it gets to the point where you started living for flyers or you're leading the single flyer for the 10th, 20th time. You're thinking, "This information is so good. Why am I giving it away for free?"

I'm sure you've been in conversations where you have one piece of advice and there's 20 newbies who say the opposite. Then because there's one of you and 20 of them, it's like you get shut down, but if you make your own product, then they can all lead out because they can't say anything in your product, right?

Kevin: Yes. It isn't like people were buying. This is a very important point.

The reason that people are buying your information product and your guides is because you take all those questions and answers and put them all in one easy-to-read guide instead of having to bounce all over to get different key points and basic information.

They're on a forum and it gets confusing but you give them the guide and explain all the steps. It makes it so much easier to people. That's what they want. People want it laid out for them.

Robert: Yes. Like you said, you get all the conversation bounced around. Even if you put that step-by-step in a forum post, then it's going to get buried on page seven and then it'll be dated 2005.

When they buy your product, they don't know how old it is or if you recently updated it and you can go back and change it. There's really no point of going back to old forum post, that's on page seven, and editing it and making it better.

Become the Author-ity

Something else that's really useful for a lot of people who hang on our forum is that they get their ideas from what people are posting on forums that you keep getting asked about. People will say, "Everyone's talking about how to make a report. Let's ask Kevin Riley."

If your name's coming up and they realize you're the person to ask for certain topics, that you only enjoy talking about on forums, it's like you're already doing it for free. You might as well get paid for it.

Kevin: It's also is where I get a lot of my ideas, and they have been really thoughtful ideas. For example, I don't know if you remember the all-times guide to using the $7 Secret System.

Robert: Yes. That sounds familiar.

Kevin: Yes. That was back in 2007 when it first came out and I liked that. It was the first time we had a system like that. I jumped on it and could see that it is a great system, but I had a hard time installing the software. Their directions were horrible. Then, I started seeing all these people in forums saying the same thing over and over in the discussions. They were having a difficult time installing $7 secrets.

I thought, "You know, why don't I create directions?" The next time I went to set up my screenshot, I did it. I put directions in and created this little guide. Because there was a definite need for this, I created and released it.

Those sales went nuts and I sold that guide for years. I updated it at some point with turn around and sold it again. It's just fantastic because I was building a need that was being voiced by people out of work.

Robert: What's cool about that is you don't have to worry about making a very good sales or making a very good thing. I think all you think about at that point, if you page set, how does it wrap, maybe like a buy-book, and that's it. You get sales.

Kevin: That was the answer I've been look for.

Robert: You probably hear this all time. People say, "What I have to teach isn't that valuable." It is. The average person doesn't know what an autoresponder is. They also don't know what Quicktag or WordPress is.

Even if someone is brand new to online marketing or if all you knew was how to get your bank tied to Google, how to write an article, how to get listed on Google Places or how to listed on Create Space, every single one of those things, are all awesome products

Sure. Someone could go to the forum. They'd get bounced around. It takes too long to look on each of your bounces, so they are willing to pay for this kind of stuff.

Kevin: An example I released quite a few years ago is the Newbie Toolcase, it tells you how to set up a blogger blog.

Anyone can do it and Blogs will show you how. It's really easy, but people want a guide. It was a big seller and I had this at high price. It's one of those $25 a rate on Linux.

In the end, I turned around and sold master seller. As I see people get hooked and list things on Amazon now, I see this with different names. People were still buying it because it's a simple guide on how to setup a blog.

It's for someone who has never been a blogger and thought it is so easy, but if you've never done it, it's not easy to them. So you might think, "Yes. That's easy. Everybody knows how to do that." But it turns out that some people don't know how and are willing to pay money for a guide to show them. It's as simple as that.

I also have one that shows people how to respond through their Gmail account. You can have a Gmail account with a guide for Vacation Responder. Everyone is on a mail slate. Mail slate is now famous.

Then people ask me what kind of software do you have? This is Gmail's Vacation Responder. It's easy. Everything was there.

Robert: Right. Now they put up that little icon and you hit that one button, right?

Kevin: Yes. It types something up and everything is there and that's the response. It'll automatically respond the same message to everybody and people don't like that. They're just like, "Why don't I just get guide about that?"

Robert: Yes. I don't know what it is, but it seems like the people who make the software are always bad at teaching it.

There are videos for GoToWebinar and they suck. Camtasia also has videos that are bad. I don't know if it's just that, they're too close to it or they don't really know who their audiences are and it's made by techies and teachers.

I know when you make your products and you make your release, you have a clear idea of who exactly it is you're talking it. It's just because you know who's having this problem that makes it way more powerful for them.

Kevin: This is why I got started in it because I noticed a lot of the persons who are really new at internet marketing that you could easily teach. I actually have a couple of years of teaching background here in Japan. I started teaching English, in my in-between time.

When construction went down before I even started getting into the internet, I was actually teaching English. People wanted me to learn English, which I found very weird.

Any Skill Can Become a Product

Anyways, it was so valuable. It was like Robert Kyosaki saying, "If you get a job, you're going to learn something about that. That provided you a practice." But the thing is, I understand from that how people learned and that's really helpful. I think if you get a chance to teach on a weekend, you might volunteer and teach one a night course.

For example, if you know how to decorate, volunteer and do a night course and teach people how to decorate cakes. That's when you see how people learn. You can bounce ideas around and learn different ways to do things.

That gets a little bit into your product relations because you realized how people learned this. It's really unique. You can even try it with your friends, teaching your friends how to do this and see how it goes.

Robert: Yes. I try to teach my girlfriend stuff all the time but she doesn't listen.

Kevin: That's different.

Robert: All right. So observe some situation and teach. You mentioned a few times that you have a report that's $7 or this thing's $5. When that whole $7 script, with a $100 commission started off, you really embraced that.

Kevin: Yes, I did. I used that back then to build my list.

Robert: At the end, that's the whole reason you do it. But before that, everyone called e vote data and suddenly it started to get scary and they didn't know what it was. It's similar to having an e-vote and if it's 50 pages, you're going to charge $15 and if it's 100 pages, you're going to charge $30. It's a PDF and it takes you 6 months to make.

But then, you had this whole $7 Scripting thing, thinking if you just got a 10-page report with screen shots, it doesn't necessarily have to be long. I just solve people's problem then, and that's all you need.

Then, if someone recommends you to get paid the whole $7, will all your products be $7 or do you have any higher priced ones? What's your strategy there?

Kevin: I don't have to sell anything at $7 or $9.95 anymore. A lot of my reports and stuff are more in the teens. I have video workshops that are a lot more and run up to $300.

I have many membership sites. So, why can't I let you do this? Really, these small guides are the beginning of the funnel. They are the ones that bring people in and because you don't know this person, you don't want to go out and buy their huge home-study course because it might not be good. But you decide to purchase the guide for a few dollars and decide to try it out.

Robert: So it's like they saw a new you from the forum. At least, they trust you enough to get you on your list. Then, they trust you enough to pay $10 and eventually they trust you enough to pay $30.

Kevin: Exactly. We came up with Instant Money Factories starting in April of 2007 and the rest started in January of 2007. By April, we were selling close to about $150 a package. The price went up pretty quick. That trust factor gave us something good and was there by April.

Robert: Yes. How much stuff do you think you have? I have new products.

Kevin: I really don't know, but I've got these new pluck worth recipes. I think there are four of them and another one coming out this month. I'm working on something today called "Pluck with Target Niche Profits." This is on targeting certain niches and it's very important that with niche. Early on, I had Plucker Blogs, which is a great membership site where people vote thorough the blogs.

Robert: Right. But it sounds like even though you have these topics all in place, it sounds like clockwork case is your brand now.

Kevin: Yes. I've been doing all these clockwork things and I'm doing consistency. I work with Clockwork Manifesto so I it will look it like a physical book. I have a real interest to avail that clockwork consistency. That's why I believe in the book business, we have to be consistent.

Robert: Again, I think you used to use recipe for whatever and then you realized you were in the chef's hat?

Kevin: Yes. On the Clockwork Recipes, I am still the chef who writes on the front cover.

Robert: That's cool. Even though it's different stuff, it's all the same? It sounds like you're working on all that stuff all the time. How often do you launch something new? Once a month, once a week, or once a day?

Kevin: It depends. Most of the time, a couple of months. When I'm working on a big project, then I might see a need for something else, then I go for that and make it and get it out there. It just depends.

Robert: It depends on how much you need to be on the forums, right?

Kevin: Exactly. I see what the need is. For example, yesterday, a new social network came out and people are having a hard time with it. So, I went and saw how they solved that problem.

Robert: For example, if someone said, "All right. How do I use Google Plus or how do I use Plurk, how much time do you think it would take you to make some kind of guide on that?

Kevin: If I were good, it wouldn't take a lot. I just do that on Facebook and save it on Facebook pages. It took me a couple of weeks to put that one out because I went way overboard. However, a lot of times, I'll just sit and get it done in three days. I think the Twitter guide was something like three days.

Robert: Is three days your average or your record?

Kevin: My record is one day.

Robert: Nice.

Kevin: It depends on how much I have to step up the screenshots. Taking the screenshots is quick and easy, and I like to set it up as examples. If I feel that in the forums, I'm putting an article to an article, I want to make the article first and then have the persons see the article out there. It's just I think much better. But that listing could take extra time. It just depends on how many examples you're going to create. Creating one at a time for new and actual screen shooting, takes a lot of time.

Robert: Yes. It's extra time but it pays off so much. We've all taken training where someone said, "Here's the first five steps."

Kevin: Yes.

Robert: Then, it was just one page or that one thing in the forum where you just get completely stuck.

Kevin: Yes. Exactly. I tried to waive that all cost so it won't get stuck, otherwise everybody will email you.

Robert: Even if you got that one question, I'm sure there are tons of other people who are just too embarrassed to ask or they just have questions and got stuck.

Kevin: Exactly. Then, it's just they emailed once.

Robert: All right. It just sounds like you're a total report creation machine. What's next for you? Are you just going to be doing more of the same or do you have some new ideas or new directions that you're going after?

Kevin: I have my new cooking website, which I'm really having fun with. That's still in the early stages. I have had it up a little bit over a month and a half, so it has recipes on there.

Robert: Are we talking recipe recipes or...?

Kevin: Yes. Food recipes.

Robert: Awesome. Is it cake decorating?

Kevin: No, it is not cake decorating. I do have to get some in there, but no. It is just some really good brownies in there right now.

Robert: The bigger ones or a special kind?

Kevin: Really special, with chocolates and nuggets, and they're melting and it's full of chocolate inside. It's really easy to make. They make them quite often and they never last.

Robert: They'd only last only a couple of minutes, right?

Kevin: They're dangerous. I got a three double rating with Dallas kitchen. The food is delicious, because you can't stop eating it.

Have Fun, Make Sales

Robert: Even with just that alone, you have a record to get down already. That's one thing that I noticed about in your marketing; in your approach is you're kind of a goofy, fun person. You really are putting a lot of personality into your stuff. I think a lot people, when they're already tired, they try to be real proper and official.

If someone came along, they would go to Camtasia or Adobe's official videos, and see that I have personality. It has a lot to do with why it makes so many sales, and why it makes so many products.

Kevin: Yes, I just have fun with it. I figured if I'm not going to have fun with it, why am I doing it? There are so many other things I'd like to do. So, if I'm not going to have fun with it, why do it?

Robert: Awesome. I think that's a perfect way to wrap this up. Have fun with what you do. You have to show what you do. So if you're going to be making an article in any way, you might as well show how you do it, with step-by-step instructions and some screen shots.

If you hang on a forum, people will keep talking about it, keep asking about it and then there's nothing wrong with showing your method, showing your way of doing it.

If you just price yourself at $9.95, use pricing routines, it makes it a really low pressure, you can just spend a few days on it and make this report with some screen shots.

Even if you think it might not be perfect or in a couple of months, you might say, "I could have made them so much better," if you put it out there and people see and like it, and they will go buy it, then it sounds like that's all that matters.

Have fun teaching something. It doesn't have to be like the encyclopedia. Just be a good teacher, right?

Kevin: Exactly, yes.

Robert: If they want to know more about crazy Kevin Riley and want to see your products, and what you're working on, where should they go?

Kevin: They go to workrecipes.com and see me and how my chef works.

Robert: That's the number one reason that I would to go, just to see that picture with the chef hat because it's priceless. This has been Kevin Riley talking to us about making products, having fun, and going after your passion. So, clockworkrecipes.com, check it out. Thanks for listening, persons.

"Build a List of One Million People" with Willie Crawford

About Willie Crawford

Willie Crawford was raised on a tobacco farm in North Carolina, living off welfare most of his youth. His family was so poor that he once wore his grandmother's shoes to school while working to earn money to replace his only dilapidated pair. This built a burning desire in Willie to break away from the cycle of poverty and build his own business.

In 1996, while still serving in the U.S. Air Force, in Hawaii, Willie decided to start his own internet-based business. By the time he retired (as a major) in 2003, Willie had built that into a 6-figure part-time income.

Willie is now one of the world's leading internet marketing, joint venture, and web site traffic generation experts, having taught at dozens of seminars in the United States, Malaysia, Singapore and the U.K. Willie has created dozens of information products, written over 1600 articles and 34 eBooks on ecommerce. He's hosted seminars, and now hosts his own radio show several times per week. Willie also owns several small software companies and even owns a web hosting company, which you'll find at http://WWW.NicheSimple.com.

Being a prolific information product creator with a knack for spotting winning product ideas, Willie has coached dozens of clients through creating and launching their own successful info products.

Willie has over 2400 websites, some of which get over 1 million unique visitors per month. Willie uses his proven traffic generation tactics to generate a steady stream of website visitors and leads for his online customers, and for local offline businesses. Willie teaches these very same traffic generation tactics at workshops and conferences.

From Zero to Hero

Willie Crawford: I've been around since the dark ages. Back in 1995-96, I was in the air force stationed in Hawaii. I was in a staff job there and we used Macintosh computers that were linked via Intranet but we also had access to the early commercial Internet. I saw people talking about making money and decided that if I stayed in the military, I wouldn't be able to start my own business.

I decided to start my first website and I never looked back. I ended up staying in the military until 2003. When I retired after 20 years, I'd built a six-figure income. I had already spoken at two seminars and hosted my first seminar, before I retired from the military. I just stumbled into it.

Robert: Do you remember what your first website was?

Willie: My first websites were on free websites. We had sites like AngelFire and there was FreeYellow.

There are a whole bunch of sites out there that would let you build a site on their domain. I put a bunch of those up and I started joining discussion lists where people were saying if you don't have enough confidence in your business or capabilities to invest in a domain name for $70 then, "Nobody's going to buy from you if you appear to fly by night." So, I went ahead and invested in WillieCrawford.com.

Later on people said, "You need to give people something to bond with you. You're all over the place." So, I threw up a cooking website where I shared some recipes from my childhood and that became my niche and my first real product was a cookbook. I wrote that cookbook and then I was on discussion forums like the Warrior Forum, and Tony Blake's forum discussing basic Internet marketing tactics. I was using list building and driving traffic and items similar to that.

I was noticed by Bob Silber who was planning a seminar in the Florida Keys. He invited me to speak and I had never been in those seminars. That was in December 2002. I said yes to Bob, and went and spoke. I hid behind the podium and read my notes. People liked it, and I became an Internet marketing expert. I thought to myself, I like this and so I started to host my own seminars. I spoke December 2002 and in April 2003, I hosted my first seminar.

I said, "I like being a big dog and a player so I'm going to start my own shopping cart system." I private labeled the 1ShoppingCart system. I took bold steps and started doing things. A lot of them fell in place - not all of them - but most of them and it was just a matter of taking action and declaring to world I'm serious about this and I'm going to do it. That's what I do.

Robert: That's awesome. One thing led to the next.

Willie: Yes. I was not an Internet marketing expert but I've read all over the place that you need to build a list and follow up with them and I thought, "Okay." I put my first list up in a subscriber form and said, "Share recipes with other people," so people were mailing their recipes and I was compiling these recipes to send them back out to the same people. Then they started asking, "Do you have a cookbook?" I said, "No, but I'll write one."

They told me what they wanted, I wrote a cookbook and it has sold steadily ever since then. I've been selling it since around 2000. I sell copies every single day and that's how simple it can be, but it was using just the basic Internet marketing stuff. I looked for a group of people with a common interest, built a database, and followed up with them. It wasn't really that complicated.

Robert: I'm sure you see this too, especially when you hang out on the forums - everyone thinks that everything needs to be super complicated and yet they don't even have the basics going on. You just mentioned with the cookbook, you have an opt-in form and a follow up sequence. I would go as far as saying 90% of people don't have an opt-in form or a follow up sequence, just a few emails to send after someone signs up.

Willie: Yes. I agree with that 100%. In fact, I've been guilty of setting up autoresponder sequence where I put in an opt-in form, invite somebody to download a free report or something and I'll only have two or three emails. After those few emails, the autoresponder sequence has died.

I look at my database, which is over a million people but I have a small list for somebody up there and all they got was two or three emails and they never heard from me again. So, that was totally wasted because I couldn't really just take them and add them to a main list because of all the different efforts.

You have to flow it out. It is a process and once you touch those people, you do really have to follow up with them. Back in the old days, we had a saying, "You follow up with them until they buy or die or unsubscribe." I still have that same belief system. If they don't tell you they're not interested, you keep following up with them. Otherwise, what's the point?

Robert: You always hear that especially on the forums. People say things like, "I'm so afraid to email my list because if I email them then they'll unsubscribe." If you don't email them then isn't it the same thing?

Willie: Yes. Whether they unsubscribe or just ignore you because you're not even talking to them, it doesn't matter. You're not making sales to them, which is the reason that you built the list. So, what's the point?

I don't mind people unsubscribing. I used to watch people who would email me after I unsubscribe from the list and say, "Why did you unsubscribe?" I said, "You actually watch who unsubscribed from your list?" I don't care who unsubscribes from my list. You get off my list, that means I wasn't providing value to you, just me cluttering up your day. So, get off my list if you don't value what I'm giving you. I'm not providing what you need on the list for and that's fine.

Email Marketing Explained

Robert: Yes. It might not be a good match but there's nothing wrong with that. How often do you contact your list?

Willie: I have lists that I email every day and I used to send a newsletter once a week and then I went to several days a week. I remember a friend, who used to mail his list in the morning and in the evening and he said, "I mail my list twice a day and they don't mind because I deliver value. I entertain them. I teach them something and they expect those emails."

Part of the problem today is that there's so much email clutter that if you don't email every day, you don't get through. There are tricks to getting through, such as letting them know that it's you by being consistent as far as the formatting and the "from" . But you have to be there to break through the noise. If you're not there a lot, you're not going to break through.

Robert: I totally agree. The way I look at it is in two ways. First of all, you have to get through because if I look at my email on any given day, there are a hundred new emails and I'm only going to see one of yours. On the other hand, I forget people if they don't email me. I'll be on people's list and they'll email me once a month, once every three months and I'm thinking, "Wait. Who are you again? How did I get on your list? Did I even sign up this?"

Willie: You need a certain volume or a certain critical mass just to be noticed in this noisy world. On the forums, they're always talking about delivering content, delivering high value, that if not every email teaches you a lesson and really train them then somehow you're violating their inbox.

I don't totally buy that either because I am in the business of selling things. So, I go and teach but I teach in a way where in every email I say that I'm selling something. It may be subtle but it's selling something. I have no problem with that, that's what I do for a living.

Robert: They say things like, "You have to teach or provide value to make it sound like it's some big grand thing," but you can teach in a couple of sentences or if the sales letter has things to say in there, that works too.

Willie: Absolutely. Every single one of my emails is a lesson on copywriting. It may be an article or maybe an invitation to a free webinar or something but it's copywriting and if you study the subtleties of it you'll go, "Wow, I see why you did that." It might be a bit pushy on why do you choose a particular word. It's subconscious now, but every single word in my emails is there for a reason. It's something I studied.

Robert: You mentioned a couple of minutes ago that your subscriber list is now over a million people. What's the secret to that?

Willie: The secret is to keep building, but you had to get other people to build your databases too. Right now, I'm focused on building the fastest list on social media. I'm using Facebook in particular because they're twice the U.S. population on Facebook. They're there and the secret is to be where they're at and to be able to get them on your list. So, I offered free reports and I have affiliate programs. Affiliates drive traffic to me but almost everything I do is focused on my number one priority: list building, so I can follow up with it.

Robert: The Facebook page, that's "The 20 Ways to Make $100,000 Online"?

Willie: That was one project I did and that was just me sitting in the backyard with a microphone talking as the birds chirped and the airplanes flew overhead. But things I actually do at the same time were not really that hard to make six-figures online. I'm probably going to stick on Amazon Kindle as soon as I put it in the right format. But for now, people could see those 20 ways and say, "Yes, I could actually make $100,000 doing this because it makes perfect sense and I get my other resources and everything."

That's building traffic but I've looked at one particular application I got from Sam Baker and I'm implementing that now. It lets you invite people to click on a "Like" button and when they click on the "Like" button it automatically subscribes them for your AWeber autoresponder, and it automatically adds them to the GoToWebinar list. It automatically posts to their wall that you like it and automatically adds them to the event page on Facebook.

As you setup this application behind the scenes, you can set it up where the next screen they get they click the "Like" button. Basically, they agree to be added to your AWeber list and they agree to be added to a list that lets them know about the webinar. So you basically added the two databases right there with just a click of a "Like" button.

They'll glance at that and go, "What am I adding myself to?" But a lot are still going to click yes. In some niches, they won't. Real estate for example, they hesitate more with that. But I'm building lists on many of the issues doing stuff like that where they're joining webinars and boom, they're in a database where they explicitly agreed to be added to a list.

Robert: So when they click the one button then it puts them everywhere.

Willie: Yes. If it's an application and you agree on the next page, "Yes, I agree to show my information and I agree to be added to a mailing list," that pulls out the email address that I use for Facebook. Most people will keep that one up to date because they want to be notified of changes on Facebook so it's their best email address. That's one of the ways I'm focused on list building because I was taught from the beginning to go to where the traffic is and that's where the traffic is.

Robert: What app are you using to accomplish that?

Willie: Sam Baker created it and I don't remember what it's called actually. He did a webinar about the folks from WebinarSwaps.com and he'd presented it there. The app itself is only $97 and he did a webinar where you can buy the app - he even bought the software, the app generator - installed it on your own domain and then turned around and offered to create the app for local businesses.

That's what I'm doing too. I'm very active in my local Glazer-Kennedy Group and my local Chamber of Commerce. I talk to the local nightclub and restaurant owners, where I've been and say, "Why don't we set you up with a fan page?" When somebody clicks the "Like" button, it lets all their friends in town know that they like your restaurant, night club, or comedy club, but it also announces who the comedian is in the next weekend."

Done For You Services

I'm charging them $1,000 to set this up and pushing that person into their AWeber account and then charge them a monthly maintenance fee.

The secret there is I bought the software for $97 that lets me create an unlimited number of apps that I charge $1,000 to set up for other people. So, the money is there.

Robert: For $1,000, you setup AWeber, fan page and then use the plugin that you already have?

Willie: Yes. I have fan page checklist, I also have a full time graphic artist in the Philippines who costs me $350 a month, and he can do anything as far as custom graphics, so it's very easy for me. Within five minutes, I can setup a fan page that will push them over to the AWeber account. It's my call to whether or not it's an AWeber account - I maintain and charge my monthly fee for maintaining that AWeber account or whether I just let them pay the regular AWeber fee. So even there, I may charge them extra for creating emails to touch those customers. It depends on what I feel like doing. I'm really towards outsourcing a lot of that too.

I have a $97 piece of software, an app generator that generates apps that I can charge $1,000 for and then I charge a monthly maintenance fee. I'm charging $300 a month to do nothing other than make sure the app is up to date, if there are changes to Facebook. But the person I bought the software from will give me the updates - I've installed them in my server.

Robert: Did you just say $300 a month to maintain it?

Willie: I deal with insurance agents, I deal with realtors, and I deal with many people. Your average small business owner is spending about $20,000 a month on advertising.

Robert: Yes, they're happy to pay it.

Willie: Yes, they are. That's the other thing is - you and I know we need to focus on the customers who have the money. That's why even though I'm known as an Internet marketer; I'm active in my local Glazer-Kennedy Group.

He introduced me to the group as the Internet marketing expert, so people come to me with all their questions and requests from all lifestyles. A lot of them are in network marketing and they ask me, "How do I get my MOM notice?" I look at it and say, "You're worth $10 million in that copy," or whatever but I show them how to stand out in a crowded marketplace using social media and they happily pay me for that. It's a good thing.

Break Out of Your Shell

Robert: I know many people especially Internet marketers are really afraid, shy or not really good at dealing with people. How did you get to the point where you're comfortable with going to seminars and dealing with business people? How do you become more of a people person?

Willie: When you become more of a people person, you notice people, you notice that we're all self-conscious and while you're wondering what they're thinking, they're wondering and worried about what you think about them and how you perceive them. When you study sociology, you study the fact that we're also self-conscious and want to be loved and appreciated.

I deal with people in a loving way the same as my children; I want to help them to be successful in business. I care about them and it's easy for me to talk to them. The first and second time I went to the Glazer-Kennedy Group in my area, I was the only black person there, the only one not in a business suit and there were only a couple of people there under 60.

I sat in the room thinking how out of place I was until the person running the meeting said, "This is Willie Crawford; he knows Frank Kern and Russell Bronson and helped them get started." I said, "Yes, Russell was asking a dumb question on the Warrior Forum and I was asked to call him a little snot." They said, "Wow, you know Russell personally?" I said, "Yes, when he first got started."

All of a sudden even though I didn't dress in a business suit everyday day, they recognized that I could help them and that's the important thing. Once they see that you can help them, they come to you.

If I have to give advice to somebody interested in getting in front of that crowd, it would be to go to your local Chamber of Commerce, ask them for a list of chamber members. It will include local organizations, like the Kiwanis. You can call the entertainment committee chair, and say, "I'm an Internet marketing expert, I've been doing this for X number of years. I'd like to come and speak at your lunchtime or dinner meeting and show your members how they can use the Internet to get more leads."

You put together a simple slide presentation, you speak, and you'll realize that what you know really does have value to these people. You pass out your business cards and they start coming to you. That's how I would do it.

Actually, I got the idea from Elsom Eldridge who wrote a book called "The Obvious Expert"; he teaches people how to position you as the obvious expert. I thought, "That makes perfect sense," and I started doing that.

Now I can speak as often as I can to local groups. You have people approaching you about spending their advertising dollars with you and they spend a lot more than the Internet marketing crowd for the same thing. That's what I'm driving right now.

Robert: That's really good advice there.

Willie: You go to the Chamber of Commerce and you say that there are more than twice as many people on Facebook as there are in the entire United States. That's where people are going. They're not going to the Yellow Pages look for things, even in the local community. They're going online and searching for it and they're hanging out on Facebook for an hour a day.

So, if you're not getting leads from Facebook, you're missing out. They think, "How do I get in front of people in Facebook?" Then you explain, "You set up a lead capture page where you offer them some bribe to get on your list," and then you automatically follow up saying, "I can set that up for you." We all understand autoresponders and maybe you'd set a series of once a week emails or once a month emails for that realtor to reach out and touch their prospects.

I go on to forums and listen to people who are writers talk about how little they are paid to write. A realtor or a doctor or a lawyer would happily pay you $75 to write a very simple article that would brand them because it's worth more in that world.

It's just realizing that what you know is worth a lot and it's just explaining it in simple terms and for those business people, its lead generation. It's about getting a customer in the door and then you'll teach them that you can help them get that customer back more by touching them automatically over and over again.

Robert: It sounds like you can be paid a lot more if you step away from everyone that's already in marketing, because they know how to write an article, and do a follow up sequence, so that skill isn't really worth that much there. But if you go to an offline business like a dentist or something, they have no idea how to write an article and now it's worth $75.

Willie: I have a friend who's charging $500 a month for publishing a newsletter for offline clients. He does it once a week. He writes up four emails a week; simple emails where the client gives most of the input and the client's paying for that. But he's also hosting on his AWeber account so if that client ever says, "I don't need you anymore," he has the client's database. So the client is not going to leave because he has the client's customers.

Some people have a problem with that but those clients don't want to learn to set up an autoresponder, set up a squeeze page. An Internet marketer would pay you $5 or $10 to do that and a local realtor would pay hundreds of dollars to do the same things. It's approaching the right people.

Robert: Awesome. It sounds like we covered lots of really cool stuff on this call. What I get from this discussion we just had was talk to people. Get yourself out more. Everything you talked about, from email your list, to hanging out in forums, talk to people face to face. Even though it is scary like you said, everyone else is just as afraid as you are.

Willie: That's humor. You just look at them and say, "Why am I intimidated?" I listened to Steve Jobs when he talked about finding out he had cancer and thinking he was going to die. He said, "I know I'm going to die anyway, so what am I afraid of? Why not take a risk and just get out there and do it."

I said to myself, just get out there, and do it. What do you have to lose? I approach the world that way. But the other point is to go where the money is. Many Internet marketers were challenged while other Internet marketers were skeptical and holding on to their money tighter and tighter and that's the wrong approach.

Ask yourself - who's has a $300,000 budget for advertising this year? Go to them and say, "Stop spending your money on cable TV commercials when it's not working. How many leads do you get from cable TV? Spend $5,000 with me and I'll get you 20 times as many leads." And they can see that.

Robert: That makes perfect sense. I'm sure everyone listening likes you after hearing from you for a couple of minutes. So if everyone wants to keep up with you and figure out what you're working on, where should they go?

Willie: They should go to my website at WillieCrawford.com. From there they can join my newsletter and I will let you know what I'm doing. They can also just Google my name, Willie Crawford and I'm on Facebook, Twitter, LinkedIn, and all those places. Everywhere I use my real name to make it easy to find me so they can connect with me.

Robert: Awesome, WillieCrawford.com. I'll definitely check you out there and on Facebook and we'll keep in touch. I really want to thank you for showing up and sharing all this great advice.

Willie: It's my pleasure, Robert, anytime. Thank you.

"Joint Ventures" with Jason Parker

About Jason Parker

Jason Parker is a pioneer list builder and business builder. Internet marketer Matt Bacak has stated that Jason Parker is directly responsible for over one million dollars in his bank account in a short about of time. He values time and health and believes in providing value, good advertising, and innovation. He likes rock n roll, country music, video games, and the NBA.

Joint Venture Traffic

Jason Parker: When I started off, I always wanted to be a copywriter and a freelancer and when I tried to be a freelancer I noticed that clients were treating me badly. They didn't want to pay top dollar so it was just like working for the man and I always hated working for other people. I thought I could make a lot more money in joint ventures than as a copywriter.

What drew me to this was working with somebody else. The reason why I say this is I've been able to make certain types of deals where I believe I've made as much or more than some of the highest paid copywriters out there, just in a different way.

Robert: And are you okay with telling me how much?

Jason: It's not measurable in the way that you think because some of the deals that I do are deals so I can get leads on my list.

Robert: You'll make a sales letter for somebody for free but then have some kind of offer that if they buy the product then they sign up to your list. Is that how you do it?

Jason: Yes. What I like to do is just write a sales letter that I think is going to be killer, I go to somebody and I say "You can use this sales letter if you want for a product that you created, all I want is an unadvertised bonus on your download page". So they have my unadvertised bonus on their download page and it goes to my squeeze page and I get those buyer leads.

Robert: And you'll go to someone who hasn't even made the product. You'll just say I made this sales letter, make a product that matches this?

Jason: They say exactly what's going to be inside it, and they can easily do it. I've never done any of those super top-secret software letters or anything crazy like that. I give them a blueprint for a product and they do it. If I know the person can generate a lot of traffic I'll go to them with a letter and try to make a deal with them. They'll see it's already written and if they like the way it looks, they're thinking in their mind this is a win-win situation, I don't have to pay this person for this letter. Instead of going to another copywriter and paying him $10,000 to write a letter, he can just pay me in leads, which he's already getting anyway. It doesn't cost him anything.

Robert: And so how often do you do this?

Jason: I did this a few times last year.

Robert: You didn't do any work, you just kind of like made a deal happen here and there and then took the cut.

Jason: Yes, I found myself a copywriter and he charged me $3,000 a letter, but I knew I was going to make much more than that from the deal, so I just gave him the money, he gave me a letter, and then we ran the letter.

Robert: I really like the strategy that you use. So you did this a few times last year and about how many new options did this get you?

Jason: I would say that I at least got 40,000 and that was 40,000 over just a few months.

Not all of them are buyers because there are different deals that we do. If you want to keep on going in the same train of thought, you can keep going on this because I can get different deals. I'll just keep on going into it if you want.

Robert: This sounds interesting, so let's keep talking about this.

Jason: So it doesn't have to be copywriting skills either because I've done this with my joint venture skills, it's just networking. I'll say, "I'll round up affiliates for you for your launch if you add my bonus to your download page, I want my bonus to be where his are, not just somewhere where it can't be found. The download page has the download links and the bonuses, and I want my bonus as a regular link right underneath it. So it's part of the package.

Robert: Did you promise a number of affiliates? How did that work?

Jason: Not really, I did it once for the rounding up affiliates because a launch is just a lot of work, and these people have so many things that they can do. If you have listeners right now who have different skills, like social media, if they wanted to create a buzz in social media and create buzz around a product launch, they could offer that skill to somebody. The key is that it doesn't cost people anything to use you.

Robert: It's nice to try them out. So these were people that you already knew because I'm just thinking, if someone has this skill, whether they have affiliates that will promote or a sales letter, or they have social media and their thinking I know who I want to contact to try this out, but how do I know that they won't rip me off. How do I know they won't just take the affiliates?

The Relationship Technique

Jason: Well it happens with relationships. The way I've always networked was I introduced people to other people and I have people introduce me to their friends, and their joint venture partners. That's the only way I think you gain trust with people is if someone vouches for you.

If you want to meet people and just climb the ladder up to the top and keep on climbing, you've just need to be introduced to other people; they have to vouch for you.

Robert: Didn't you have some kind of system where you introduce me to five people or something like that?

Jason: Yes, they call it the five for five method. I'll go to some of my top members or partners and I'll say, "I'll introduce you to five of my joint venture partners if you do the same for me."

Then you just keep on doing the same thing, network and be friendly with people. I will actually do favors for other people and so when the day comes that I need to cash in my chips, I'll go to them and they'll remember all the good I've done for them. Plus I like meeting people.

Robert: That's something that many people neglect, including me. It's really easy to be on your computer, not pick up the phone, make your products, and mail your list but who can say no to 40,000 options. If you have the right kind of connections then you can have as big a list as you want and as many sales as you want. I know that this recording is going to be really helpful to many listeners because I hear it over and over. They'll make a product and I'll know that they need to get affiliates and need to get JVs (joint ventures). They'll go and make the sales letter better or they'll go and write more auto responders but I tell them "You just need to have one good person to recommend you and the way to do that is relationships."

The way I see many people do things is they'll say, I'll mail for you and you mail for me, then you'll see thirty people mail the same person and then he has to mail thirty different people the rest of the year. But I really like this system of I'll do this thing for you in exchange for my bonus. Even if that ends up being 100 opt-ins, or 1,000 opt-ins, that's 1,000 opt-ins you wouldn't have had.

Jason: What's interesting about the you mail for me and I'll mail for you thing, I've figured out a way to build some chips to cash in without mailing for somebody and that is to just connect them with your own network. If you build this network and you connect them with your network, it's as if I've just handed them a pot of gold. It's as if I've made him $1,000 or $2,000. You can build up your chips that way and then cash them in later.

Robert: What do you mean by that? What do you mean by connecting them with your network?

Jason: Well, you build your network up the way I was talking about, as far as introducing and being introduced to people, then when you meet somebody new and you like them and if someone else has vouched for them, then you just plug them into all the people you know. You are doing something good for them.

Robert: You can tell them that you know a copywriter and you're going to hooky them up with him but now you owe me. In the end, I didn't have to give up my subscribers.

Jason: Yes, it doesn't really feel like I'm doing it out of the goodness of my heart, you're just hooking people up.

Robert: Right.

Jason: And I know that they like me now as well.

Robert: It's not really like a one to one, not like you scratch my back I'll scratch yours, it's that you're helping as many people as possible. You know that some of that is going to come back to you. You might recommend this copywriter or this social media person to a product creator and they might do something together and never come back to you and that's fine. You're just making a habit of having this network and you'll have some favors too when you need them.

Jason: Yes, I know a graphic designer that needed some work so I plugged him in to 40 different people. He got a bunch of work and now he likes me. You know what I mean? He might introduce me to someone down the road who might be key in my business.

Robert: And that's cool too.

Jason: Now he'll be more responsive to anything I bring to him. This is the key man, the key to networking really is, and many people approach it like they want to take, take, and take. However, if you just give, give, give instead then it builds up this trust and they'll read the emails that you send them. If you ever need anything you can go to them, they'll remember the thing you've done for them and the value you've given them just freely, they'll like you, and they'll read exactly what you tell them.

Robert: I mean, because you've sent me thousands of email subscribers, now Lance and I just say all right whatever Parker wants we'll set it up for him.

Jason: It's so cool.

Robert: You have this because it works on both sides, right? If one person is look for a graphic designer, you helped that person out, now he has a graphic designer, but you also helped the graphic designer because now he has a job.

Jason: Yes. It's just all about helping and providing value. I mean business is just about providing value period. If you just think about it.

It's the same thing with your customers, or anybody you want to meet and network with. I know people have referred to me as the Networking King and stuff to their friends. You hooked me up with more people than anybody else has ever done. I don't really feel like I am the life of the party or anything like that but I just feel around and I connect people together and it's a form of gaining trust with people and getting people to like you.

Robert: Have you ever thought about systematizing it? Because I'm sure these people have whole membership sites, where if you want a joint venture you just join this site and then they'll figure out who to connect you to. If you want to be the network person, have you thought about something like that?

Jason: The only problem with this skill is that nobody cares about it. We know the value of it but if you were to go out to the masses and say hey you want to learn how to network, you're not going to sell anything.

Copywriting is not a big thing that the masses are going to buy, but you and I know that it's the life force behind your business in many ways.

Robert: Joint Ventures are number one, number two is copywriting, but everybody just wants to know how I make articles, and how I make products? They feel as if the big gurus make all their money because they have a good sales letter and they know everyone who will promote them.

Jason: That's exactly right. I can build a case for how you need this but it doesn't make people want it. That's the only problem with my special skill, copywriting; if no one wants my special skill, I'm pretty much screwed.

Robert: Yes. However, isn't that all you need? What's stopping you from making a package that includes someone who will make your product, another to make your graphics, and someone to make your sales? What's stopping you from making like a $2,000 package with all of this stuff built in?

Jason: Yes, that's a good one. I think about it sometimes. I use my skills in different ways; people want the plug and play, so I'll write some copy and put it on the squeeze page so they can use that. However, the one point I wanted to make, there is one more tactic about copywriting and joint ventures.

You should tell some who already has a product, "You should write this letter as if you've already done this interview with somebody and sell the interview for $7 or if it's good, sell it for $17. You tell the person I want to interview you and I'm going to sell this interview. It's going to be a paid interview so he can cut loose and teach what he wants; he doesn't have to hold back. The bottom line is you're going to sell their product on your download page.

Robert: Is this an up sell or is this a bonus?

Jason: This can be just something you promote from your download page. You have complete control over the product, like you own it.

Robert: By download page, do you mean that have they bought, or have opted in?

Jason: They have to buy. He might promote the actual page to sell the interview. That's a good way to use your copywriting skills by selling this interview full of great stuff. You might want to add it as a bonus or something to beef it up. It's possible that only 10% of the people who actually buy on the front end will order their product on your download page.

Brokering

That's another way to use your copywriting skills. You don't actually have to create the stuff. Here's the thing, I'm good at copywriting, good at networking and I'm good at list building but I do that through networking and copywriting.

I'm not good at the things that people want. For example, people want certain traffic tactics. I'll go to somebody who knows that stuff and I'll interview him and then write the sales page for that. So I don't have to be the expert at it, I don't have to pretend to be an expert in something I'm not an expert in.

Robert: Right. I can't stand when you see people make a product and you can just tell that they watched a video or read someone else's product and really taught it. You should go to the original person, interview him and then he's done most of the work for you and then you're doing the promoting, and you're the person that makes it happen. You know what, it's almost like you're holding your own miniature seminar but instead of a seminar it's online, and it's just one speaker.

I mean some of these people running seminars, are idiots right? They put the seminars together by getting the speakers, who do all the teaching, promoting, and sales. Then they are being paid for bringing it all together.

Jason: Yes, that's pretty much what it is. If you're a good copywriter or something, you do it smartly.

Robert: Do it smartly, there you go. So when is your traffic interview product coming out?

Jason: I don't know. This is something I fool around with every so often. The other day, there was a person who wanted me to make this product for freelance copywriters but, I'm not doing it. I know that copywriters for some reason don't like to work for other people. I don't know why. It'd make me just crazy to work for someone else.

Robert: Well, because maybe they're not marketers, they don't have a list and would rather just be paid.

Jason: Yes, that's true. Here's another thing. If I was starting all over and I was good at copywriting, I would just go to somebody who creates products, has a list, has the traffic and I would just go on a rampage creating products with them. He would create the product and I would write the sales page repeatedly. By taking just a percentage, I work with him not for him.

Robert: Yes, I've made that kind of deal before and it's a lot of fun.

Jason: You don't have to take anything off the front end either, you can make it more lucrative for him by having him keep 100% of the front end and I would take 50% of the up sell.

Robert: OKAY. We're running out of time, but how did you get so good at copywriting?

Jason: I don't have enough time doing it to be a master, a true master. I found out there are no shortcuts.

Robert: Did you have to write your own sales letters? Did you read certain books, or take courses to learn how to write sales letters?

Jason: I studied everybody from Michel Fortin to Gary Halbert, and Eugene Schwartz. I don't try to create any copywriting products; these persons already have the information out there. I've spent about $500 a month on my copywriting education. Because I know that my future and my business depends solely on my ability to sell. You know, if I have this one skill, I can sell.

Robert: Yes, I know you go to seminars every now and then. Every time I go to a seminar I always come across a person who says they have a really great idea, I'm not going to tell you what it is but let's JV, I'll get 50% just for the idea and then we'll do it. I'm thinking, "No, you bring some kind of a skill and by that I mean you make the sales letter, bring in the list or make the product. Just having the idea is not going to do it, ideas are good but you also have to bring a skill to the table." Copywriting is one of the highest paid ways to be a writer and if you're good at it, it's a lot of fun too.

Jason: You know what's funny; they think the copywriters have all the power like the copy has the power. You know people will go and hire copywriters but really, copywriters should just go and hire product creators.

Robert: Right, it never works that way though right?

Jason: It never does. Why would you work for someone else and make just 5% of what they make. You just made them loads of money. People don't realize that everything depends on that. The people who have all the traffic are the ones who have good copy.

Robert: Right, because if someone is going to buy a product they can't actually see the product, all they have to base it on is the sales letter. I think the reason they don't do that is that they hear about your cool tactic of writing the sales letter and taking a bonus or a percentage of the up sell. They just didn't know about your secret strategy.

Jason: Yes, you know, I've never talked about it except once or twice, here and there. People aren't normally interested but I thought your buyers would be because they're serious business owners.

Robert: And you can't discount where one new connection leads. You know what I mean? I've run an interview with some person that led to a recommendation from someone else, which led to a product with someone else, which led to some huge affiliate, you never know.

I mean whatever your skill is, a copywriter, a graphic designer that still works, making products, doing a webinar, getting affiliates, getting traffic, or building a list. What I keep getting at is just help someone and see where it leads. Interrupt their pattern; everyone is used to seeing people promote this thing for 50% or I'll mail for you if you mail for me. What if you took your skill like Jason is saying and you go to someone who needs it, who pays a lot for copywriting, who needs a better sales letter, a product or needs a bonus and just say here is the deal, I want to lay it out for you.

Instead of the same old thing, I'm going to give you this service, I'm going to add this bonus to you, and then you can include this as part of a product. One other thing that I think we skipped over a bit, that everyone really needs to apply when it comes to offline events and networking is the five for five strategy. This means that you find, through normal networking, five people that you can introduce to someone new. Then tell them, "I've got copywriters, graphics designers, persons with email lists and I want to introduce you to these five people. Now do you have five people that you could introduce to me?"

It's so easy to think; you help me, give me, give me, give me, but if you're more of a giving person and you introduce people here and there and see where it leads, a lot of times you can build up this good will and cash in your chips. You can hooky someone up with a graphic designer, or a programmer and then what happens later on when it comes time to do a launch and you're asking people do you want to promote this, then they have a much more likely chance, just because you introduced them to some new person.

So Jason is there a website where everyone listening can monitor you and see what you're up to, what your latest and greatest stuff is?

Jason: Yes, you can check out our company website named ES3MarketingLLC.com.

There is a good copywriting article on there if you want to check that out. I like to keep things behind the scenes Robert, so you never know what I'm behind.

Your Blog, Membership Site, Email List...
Making Money Online Automatically and...
It's All Done in Under 3 Days

I'll want to get you on the right track to having all this setup within the next 3 days or less:

- Niche & Domain Name
- Blog & Social Proof
- Web Host & Web Page
- Sales Letter & Payment Button
- Email Optin Page
- Membership Site & Drip Content
- Autoresponder Messages
- Traffic

Even in the fancy $2,000... $3,000... even $10,000 courses... teach USELESS skills that are WAY over your head:

- "Now that you have an optin page, I forgot to tell you... you need a blog"
- "Now that you have a blog, I forgot to tell you... you need a sales page"
- "Now that you have a sales page, I forgot to tell you... you need a product"

Sound familiar? Nothing takes you from start to finish... in just one easy weekend, until now:

http://www.IncomeMachine.com

"Scaling Your Business" with Stu McLaren

About Stu McLaren

Stu McLaren is the Co-Founder of WishList Products, whose passion for building online communities served as the catalyst for the development of the membership platform WishList Member. Today he uses WishList Member for his own membership sites as well as to serve the charity he co-founded with his wife called World Teacher Aid (www.WorldTeacherAid.org).

WishList Member

Stu McLaren: I am a person who wanted to run my own business and spent a long time figuring out what that business would look like. The business evolved into a software company where we developed a piece of membership software called WishList Member.

The primary reason we actually developed it in the beginning was that I needed it for my own purposes. I am not very technical, but one of the things that I was struggling with was being able to get my own membership site up and off the ground. I collaborated with a good friend of mine, named Tracy Childers and we developed WishList Member. Lo and behold, there were a lot of other people around the world that were look for a similar type of solution and it now powers over 27,000 online communities and membership sites.

That has provided me a wonderful opportunity to build the business I always wanted and at the same time gave me the freedom to be able to pursue some other interests as well. As you mentioned, my wife and I also have our own charity called World Teacher Aid where we bring education to different parts of Africa. One of the benefits of having your own business is being able to do some cool stuff like that as well.

Robert: It sounds like you keep busy.

Stu: I definitely try to. We just had our first child as well, little Marla, she also keeps us very busy as well.

Robert: That's a cool way to make software because I see people all the time and they'll think of some random silly idea or they'll look at what everyone else is doing and try to copy it. So, what you did was say, "I have this need and I'm going to be using this software anyway, so I might as well create it. Not only will I have the software itself but now I also have something to sell."

Stu: I think that's the best way to make software. When you need for it yourself, you're going to be much more in tune with designing something that users are going to get benefit from. When you're designing for somebody else, it can be challenging because you're always trying to put yourself in their shoes but when you're designing for yourself, you know when you're going to like certain things and if there are enough people out there that are similar to you, you're going to have a winning combination.

I always like designing software that we use and in fact, every piece of software that we've developed in this company has been because we have had a need ourselves. I think that that's a much more solid base to work from than it is trying to come up with something just because.

Robert: What makes WishList unique is when I look at the interface, the terms you used, and the way the tabs are laid out, it really looks like you put a lot of thought into it. I don't want to badmouth any other membership software but when I look at many of these other solutions, it was like throwing on the side, throwing it on the bottom, and the program started adding to it.

Not only did you make it but then you actually used it and you went back and said, "It makes more sense to have this thing over here and have these buttons over to the side." You can tell there's a lot of thought was put into making it dummy proof.

Stu: We always joked that we're like the hair club for men. We not only created the product but we use it ourselves too. You're right in the sense that we're using it all the time. I think through that, we see ways that we can improve it. In fact, we've just finished a massive overhaul on the user interface again and we've added some other very cool features. It comes as a result of using it day in and day out and we see ways that it can be improved.

I think as you mentioned there are other companies and other solutions, but they're not coming from the same perspective. They're designing for somebody else their not actively using it themselves and therefore, they can never truly put themselves in a user's position. We're very fortunate in the sense that we have a great piece of software where it serves a purpose in our business, and fortunately, many other people like it too.

Robert: For some internet marketers it's easier to make more money by making a new product every week or every month than by going back in overhauling and redesigning stuff. What you have done, is have the same product for several years, which goes against the grain. I've seen many newbies, make product after product and then they get tired. Was that your intention to have just one big product and keep sticking with it?

Stu: When I look back, Robert, I don't know that we anticipated that WishList would be a big as it is. We knew that there was a demand in the market, but it's really blown us away. We do very, very well in terms of the number sites. When I look back, a year ago, I we had 7,500 online communities and memberships were powered by WishList Member and now fast forward a year and we're over 27,000. In a year's time another almost 20,000 sites are now being powered by this software and it just continues to grow in that phase.

I think it was a happy accident for us in the sense that because it grew so quickly, we were forced in a way to channel all of our resources, time, energy and effort to one product. In hindsight, that has been a tremendous benefit because I think the reality of the situation is you outline as people jump from one project to the next.

The downside to that is that you never really get to refine the product itself, but not only that, the sales process. Many people setup a sales letter, they'll drive some traffic to it through Pay-Per-Click and then they forget about it and move on to the next thing. They don't focus on tweaking the sales letter and optimizing it to the best conversion and modifying the sales process so that you can maximize sales, improving the product, staying connected with those customers, and look for ways that you can improve it so forth.

Just through the sheer necessity of keeping up with the demand and supporting the product, we've been forced to focus on that one issue. As a result, it really opened my eyes to the fact that we as business owners get so much more benefit when you really look to build a business around one particular product. It doesn't mean that you can't develop other products, but at the same time, it just proves that whenever you're going to introduce a new product, we really put forth the effort to maintaining it on an ongoing basis, improving not only the product but the sales process and then certainly stay in tune with customer base.

Avoiding That Support Nightmare

Robert: Let's talk about that because everyone I know who gets involved with software has a complete nightmare with it. It's fun to make a report or make some videos because the only real customers you have there is when someone says, "My payment didn't go through," or "I can't get access." However, when you have software, it's like a double edge sword because it's easy to get people to want it, to like it, to get the appeal but once they get it, they don't always know the interface or it's not compatible.

Can you talk for a second about how you deal with all the support since you have admin? You said you've tripled in the past year, so how have you dealt with all the extra customer support?

Stu: It was a learning process for us, Robert. Truthfully, it's a pain in the butt because the way our software works is that people can install it on their own server. Because of that, you have a whole set of complications that come into the mix because everybody has a different type of server. Some are on cheap, shared hosting accounts like GoDaddy that are not conducive to this type of software and then you have people that are on virtual servers, mail servers and dedicated servers. Everybody has different settings and are using a different WordPress theme.

There are all kinds of complications that come up at any one point - one setting, one little tweak in a theme or whatever could throw things off. Therefore, it was definitely a learning curve for us in terms of managing all of that. One of the things that we've learned though is because our software is based on WordPress; we have put forth a concentrated effort to ensure that our products are compatible with WordPress development standards and every new version of WordPress that comes out.

From that point forward, we've been very fortunate, as we've grown, we've added more people. I think we now have 15 full-time people and over half of our company is developers and then the other half, in some way, play some type of a support role. Therefore, it's a very fine balance. Whenever you develop a product like this, you have to have a team in place to support it because people will have questions.

There are things you can do to reduce that. You can make sure your product is always compatible to the latest versions of WordPress or whatever type of software you're using. However, more importantly, you want to be proactive in your support. You want to think through as a new user what would be the first step that somebody would go through to use this. What questions are they going to have? How can we answer those ahead of time with other support videos and knowledge base? Can we make ourselves available for support by having pre-answered questions in advance?

One of the things we added just within the last year was a setup wizard because again, we knew when somebody installed WishList Member the first question was, "Now what?" So, the setup wizard walks them through the basics of setting up their site.

There are things that you can do when you're developing software to make it easier for the user. The key is putting yourself in their shoes, thinking through what questions they're going to have and trying to answer them before they have to ask. But at the end of the day, people are always going to have questions and you need to have a team in place to help answer them.

In the beginning, it was Tracy, my business partner, Mike, my other business partner and I - there were the three of us and we were answering all the questions. As more and more sales came through, we had the capability to add more and more people to the point now where coming up three years later we have 15 full-time people to support our customers. It's always an ongoing battle in terms of making a product that doesn't need support but at the same time providing support when people do need it.

Robert: One thing that you people are awesome with is having the support ticket system too. You mentioned Tracy, I was talking to Tracy a few years ago and he said, "I was having trouble with this one plugin you sold and I was trying to get support and I couldn't find the help desk."

I told him, "I tried the help desk a few years ago and people would email me on the help desk and email another copy over email."

He said, "Dude, put the help desk back in," because he has a software called FLV Producer. He said, "I haven't even logged into the help desk in two years because I have someone who handles it."

What's cool is if I have some kind of issue with WishList, I can put in a ticket and it is assigned to someone, and if it needs to be assigned to someone else, they respond to me and then passes it along. It's really a cool way for them to manage all that stuff.

Stu: It allows you to scale and I think that's the most important piece because if you don't have systems in place that allow you to grow and to get bigger then you're going to be limited by your own capabilities. We want to build a business that provides us flexibility and freedom. We don't want to create a business that's going to bog us down. A support desk is the fastest and easiest way to help manage ongoing support.

Train Your Customers

From that point on, it's about training your customers in terms of the steps to take. So we encourage our customers to look through and watch the videos because they clearly explain how to use it. We encourage customers if they have further questions to look at the knowledge base second because chances are; any additional questions have already been answered.

If they still have, questions specific to their situation they can contact us through the support desk and we are available Monday thru Friday, 9:00 AM to 6:00 PM EST. We have a team of people that are there to help answer any questions. But from a business owner's perspective, the support desk definitely allows you to grow because now you can add additional people who can help answer tickets accordingly.

Robert: Since we're talking about adding people in and scaling, I'm curious about how you started? We were talking about all the cool stuff that you've setup. You have this idea for this WordPress Membership plugin but you didn't do any of the coding, right?

Stu: No. I am not a coder. The way that worked was I went into Photoshop and I started designing what I envisioned an awesome membership solution would look like. Then our lead developer, Mike Lopez took the screens that I developed and made it all work. Mike was the mastermind behind the code.

From that point forward, it was cumbersome to continue using Photoshop if we wanted to make any changes. We now use a program that has dramatically sped up the production of other plugins and software applications that we develop and this is called MockFlow. The thing about MockFlow is that it gives people the ability to create interfaces and mockups that developers can use to develop the actual software. You can find the program at MockFlow.com

Many times what will happen is you know somebody who's very skilled at developing code but may not necessarily be skilled at design so it gives them something to look at and work from and it actually speeds up the production of the development. At the same time, it gives somebody like me who's not necessarily skilled at all when it comes to developing code a way to be able to visually outline what I would like to see and then have it developed accordingly.

We use MockFlow all the time in our business. It's something that is continuously being used as we develop new plugins, add new features and so forth. We design it and then we hand it over to our developers and they develop it.

Robert: So you made up this mockup and then you gave it to Tracy and then Tracy got Mike to code it. Is that how it worked?

Stu: Yes. Both Tracy and I worked with Mike in terms of making sure that we had the different features that we wanted included in the first version of WishList Member. It took us a couple of months to finally get it ready. We had a beta for about a month and a half after we started and then we had a beta group that tested it out for us for about a month. Then we finally sold it to the public a few weeks after that.

From that point forward, a lot of the tweaks that were made and continued to be made are based on user feedback but also through our own experiences of using it every day ourselves and seeing where people are getting stuck and what we can do to eliminate those challenges and roadblocks.

Robert: Awesome. As you are getting that feedback and improving it, what's next for you?

Stu: We see a couple of other opportunities in terms of additional products that could be developed. We like to take things a little bit slow in terms of our decision to pull the trigger on new products because we want to be able to put forth the energy and resources to make sure that they're going to be rocking just like WishList Member.

We have a big update coming out with some exciting new features that will be released with a whole redesign of the user interface. Our goal is to continue to support people who are building online communities and membership sites and finding ways to make their live easier by creating additional tools.

Robert: Awesome, that's great. We went over so many things and I want to really quickly recap for everyone listening.

What happened with Stu was he and Tracy and Mike put out an awesome product called WishList Member, which is membership software for WordPress. He had this idea and he knew how he wanted it to look but he wanted an effective way to communicate to others how to put it together.

He used Photoshop and designed the perfect membership solution to use. Then he gave it to Tracy, had Mike code it up and then they made this simple membership solution that's easy to use and it was the software that they were going to use every day in their business anyway. He also uses a tool called MockFlow.

If you see a hole that's not being filled, or if you're experiencing frustration whether it's with something online like a membership software, an iPhone app, any kind of product where something needs to exist for you, then it really helps for you to make it as if it's something you would use. That way, you're your own case study because you can just use this every day and find out the way that you want to use it. You can also send it off to your customers and get feedback from them and figure out where they're being hung up.

It's nice if you have software that's a big hit. It's tempting to say, "Oh great, I just did this launch. I have a bunch of money coming in. Let me go and start from scratch." If you have a big hit, keep it going and refine it and make the next version.

One thing that is always tough when you scale is customer support. Stu and Tracy have made sure to get ahead of the customers' questions. They've made excellent customer support videos, manuals and a knowledge base.

Even though a certain plugin or a certain piece of software makes sense to you, it might not make sense to someone who's just starting out. So, make support materials so that anyone who is brand new to your software likes it, loves it and it doesn't take a bunch of your time or you don't have to take a bunch of their time to actually use it.

Stu has a software company called WishList Member. For most people, they'd say, "The business is going to grow and explode and get 200 employees." What Stu wants to do is make sure that the membership software that he has continues to run, continues to be easy to use. They're making add-ons for it instead of doing what most typical programmers do and adding a bunch of stuff, that nobody needs. They're adding things that everyone does need and they have an awesome product.

Stu, where can people go to find out more about you and get WishList Member?

Stu: You can go check out WishList Member by going to www.WishListMember.com and if you want to see some of the stuff that we're doing with the charity, you can go visit www.WorldTeacherAid.org.

"Copywriting for Beginners" with Ryan Healy

About Ryan Healy

Ryan M. Healy is "The Most Referred Direct Response Copywriter on the Internet." Since 2002, he's worked with 75+ clients, including Alex Mandossian, Terry Dean, and Pulte Homes.

What's more, Ryan has written hundreds of sales letters, crafted thousands of emails, and discovered what really works to bring in new customers and bigger profits.

Because he helps business owners get better results from their advertising, he focuses his creative efforts on writing online sales letters, email messages, direct mail letters, and space ads for newspapers and magazines.

Ryan is the co-author of the book Million-Dollar Marketing Secrets, and frequently publishes articles about how to write sales copy and advertisements on his blog, and on hundreds of web sites on the Internet.

In fact, Ryan has published multiple articles on Michel Fortin's blog; been referenced multiple times on Terry Dean's blog and in his print newsletter; and is a regular contributor on the BoostCTR blog and Charlie Cookay's Marketing for Success blog.

Ryan lives in Denver, Colorado. He's been married to Stephanie since 1999 and has three children.

Making Money

Ryan Healy: I have been a freelance copywriter for over nine years. The first three years though I was employed and the last six years I've been freelance.

Robert: Who employed you?

Ryan: It was a home schooling company and I wrote copy for their annual catalog, website and sent out emails and so forth although the nature of the writing I was doing for them was quite a bit different from the style of writing that I do now.

Robert: You didn't need to do a price drop in the home schooling newsletter?

Ryan: I actually did. It wasn't a price drop, it was buy this microscope before we raise the price and we sold lots and lots of microscopes.

Robert: A price scarcity then?

Ryan: Yes.

Robert: You did that and then you decided I'm good at this I want to do more of it, I want to get paid more, work for myself and then you started freelancing?

Ryan: That probably would have made more sense than what I did. I've always been entrepreneurial and wanted to work for myself and I've always had things on the side. What I was doing when I worked at Sunlight was two things. I went through the AWAI Copywriting Course, which taught how to write long form sales letters.

I was going through that but I was also getting my "Series 6" registration or "Series 6" license so that I could be a financial planner. I set up a deal with this other person who was successful. He told me he was making half a million a year in commissions so I thought he would be a good person to learn from and we set up this relationship. When I got my annual bonus, I quit my job and became a financial planner and that was on April 19 2005, one month after my second child was born.

From then until June 13, I made $200, so the whole deal I had with him was falling apart and nothing was working as I expected it to. I had a little money left in my bank account, which was going to be enough for about two weeks, and I said I've got two options. I can get a job or, since I just finished this course on how to write sales letters, I could go freelance. I love writing copy, I've always wanted to be a writer so let's go for it and that's what I did. I got three clients the first week and just kept going ever since. It would have made more sense to quit and launch my copywriting business but that's not what I did.

Robert: I deal with so many people who want to make a bunch of money and I always tell them to start by just getting hired by someone. If it means you have to pick up the phone and call someone or someone calls you, it might be scary to say pay me a grand or two grand to write this sales letter, but you've got to start somewhere and that's where the fast money is.

Ryan: Exactly. And that's exactly what I did. I picked up the phone. I was using a website called Direct Response Jobs and there were a few jobs posted there. I didn't have enough time to submit to this website and wait and see if people are going to reply back, if they had a phone number I called them and that's how I got the first job. I caught the person on a cell phone, and I started talking to him and he said, "What would you charge for a sales letter?" I didn't know so I said $1,000 and he said okay and that was that. A thousand dollars for his sales letter.

Robert: Sounded pretty simple?

Ryan: Yes.

Robert: So those three jobs got you through the first month and that was how you got your jobs? You went to that website, found the phone numbers and gave them a call?

Ryan: I got two out of the three that way. One of the things I noticed was people were always dropping off flyers on my door for painting services, house cleaning services, and sometimes I'd get postcards in the mail for similar types of things and I thought these flyers are terrible. I could rewrite one of these flyers and it would do much better.

I called three or four different people and one of the women was a Hispanic woman and she had a house cleaning business. She was doing OKAY but she was putting these flyers under doors that had misspellings, it was terrible. I thought this woman needs a better flyer so I called her and she actually agreed and I charged her $200 or $250. She wrote me a check upfront, and I rewrote the flyer for her. When she used that flyer, she was got twice as many callbacks and more work as well. She told me that she was thrilled. It cost her one or two house cleaning jobs to pay me but then after that it was all gravy.

I got clients by calling people who were already marketing to me. I used my relationship to them as a way to break the ice. I'd call up and say my name is Ryan Healy and I'm a neighbor of yours and I just got your flyer. I was looking at your flyer and it's good but I have some ideas that might generate a better response for you. Would you be interested in talking about that and usually they say yes. It's an easy way to break the ice with people by saying you're their neighbor.

Robert: They're not going to hang up on their neighbor?

Ryan: Correct.

Robert: You tell them do they want to increase the response and they say yes, then what do you say?

Ryan: I would say I have some ideas for rewriting your flyer using a better headline and maybe crafting a stronger offer but I kind of flowed with it. The better thing to do is try to get them talking to you. If you can get them talking to you that's better, you want to be focused on what their problems are. If they already think they're getting enough business from their advertising then you may as well not push it too much because if they don't perceive they have a problem then you can't help them, right?

Robert: Right and nothing is going to close them.

Ryan: That's what I did. I asked them how well it was performing for them and they would tell me. Sometimes I would ask them how many flyers they distributed because in the flyer business you get print runs of 500, 1,000, 2,000 so they know exactly how many flyers they've had printed. I would ask them how many flyers did you get printed and distributed and they'll say a thousand. I ask when you give out a thousand how many phone calls do you get and they'll sometimes say five. I say does that turn into business for you and they might say that one out of five will. Then you say, I can't make any promises but I think that I could increase that number for you just by rewriting your flyer and you take it from there to see how they respond.

I was surprised. In the online world with savvy marketers if you ask what their response rate is and what keywords are you bidding, they'd probably be gun shy because they don't want to give up data. In the offline world, a lot of those entrepreneurs and business owners who are in the service business know their numbers to a degree and they're not bashful about sharing them either.

Robert: It's cool too because a lot of the offline persons don't know what a headline is or what an autoresponder is and all these things that seem basic to us is new and exciting to them, right?

Ryan: Right. It's all new and exciting to them. One of the reasons I went after that was because I looked at it and said I can't fail. How can I create a flyer that does worse than the one I already have?

Robert: You'd have to work at that.

Ryan: Yes, I'd have to work at it so it was very low risk to me and it was great to "get real world practice" and get paid for it. I wouldn't necessarily try to build a business on that long term but in the short term, you can get a few nice jobs from it. They're all low risk, easy to finish and quick paydays.

I actually did the numbers and I think this is pretty important for anybody who is going to quit their job is you've got to figure out how much you were making every day at your job which I think, if I'm remembering how you do that, you take your annual income and divide it by 250. Is that right?

Robert: Yes, that sounds right.

Ryan: Divide by 250 and that tells you how much money you make in a day. Back when I quit my job, I was making around $230, $240 per day so to make $250 off a flyer that it only took me an hour or two to make is great.

Robert: With your day job, were you commuting or were you working from home?

Ryan: I was commuting.

Robert: That factors into it too.

Ryan: It was eight hours or eight and a half hours of work but then at various times my commute was half an hour one way so would add an extra hour per day.

Robert: You could commute for an hour a day to this job or spend an hour a day on this flyer and make the same amount of money?

Ryan: Yes.

Robert: You said when you got started most of what you were doing was flyers or was it flyers and long form copy?

Ryan: Yes, it was long form copy for the first few clients I had. One client had a steady stream of work for me, which turned out to be good. I landed him as a client the same way as the others by calling him up because he had posted his phone number and said he was looking for a copywriter.

After that, I started going to seminars because I was ready to do whatever it took to succeed. I had heard it made sense to go to a seminar and network and get copy jobs that way. I went to a big seminar in fall of 2005 and I traced that single event to over six figures in copywriting fees.

I don't think I've ever been to a seminar where I did better than that but at every seminar I went to I was able to get at least one client and I think the least amount I ever made by attending a seminar was $8500.

Robert: You've got a good system going?

Ryan: Yes. At marketing seminars there are other marketers and people who are actually running businesses online, they need people to write copy for them. Now some people write all their own copy and that's fine, but some people don't. Some people are too busy running their businesses and they outsource it and those are the people, as a copywriter, you're most interested in, especially the ones who are savvy about online marketing. If I was getting the same fee from a person who was new to online marketing or direct response marketing and a person who had some experience, I would definitely want to work for the person who had some experience.

You don't have to train them and he realizes I'm a copywriter. A new person may think you write the sales letter and then that's it, I'm done, and I'm going to make a ton of money. Well there are a lot of other things than making money. Copy is one piece of it but you've got to have email, traffic list and other things.

Robert: Is that what you've been doing since then? Is that where your new jobs come from, by going to seminars now?

Ryan: I did that for the first couple of years. I would go to one or two events a year. One of my strategies really has been to take care of the clients that I have and make sure that I'm doing a good job for them or the best job that I can possibly do for them.

There is a kind of dichotomy as a freelancer. When you get a copy job, you have to do the work but you also have to look to see where your next job is coming from. If all you did was work on that job and didn't market yourself, then you would be stuck. Even though that person loved your work if he didn't, have any more work for you and you weren't doing any marketing, now you would have nothing to do and you're scrambling to market yourself.

My strategy over time has been to get testimonials and referrals from clients. There was a period of time where I got many clients through AdWords advertising. I wrote a sales letter, posted it on my website and sent outwards traffic to that website. The website didn't collect any money it just asked them to contact me to talk about copywriting.

Building Up a Client Base

I built up my client base through a combination of things. The first few weeks it was calling people who either expressed a need for a copywriter or believed they had a need for a copywriter and that's where my first jobs came from.

Then I moved into seminars and I used seminars for a period of two to three years and then I added on top of that. I started in June and I didn't even get my website up until September and then I didn't like what I'd written, so I rewrote everything in January of 2006 and I started selling AdWords sometime in 2006 and that became the strategy I was using. All these snowballed. I didn't want to rely on any single method because what if one method didn't work very well or what if one method worked one or two months and all of a sudden, it stops working as well? I've seen that happen over time. Certain strategies have worked better at different periods of time for me.

I did that and then in 2006, I started a blog on TypePad, as well, which is still up. I wanted to start blogging as a copywriter and demonstrate that I knew what I was talking about because what's better? Going out and chasing clients or having them come to you?

Robert: Come to you.

Ryan: Yes. I thought chasing clients is fine, if you have to do it, you have to do it. Everyone has to start somewhere so that's where I got started. I thought it would be better if I can build up my authority in this space so that clients begin to come to me. They'll recognize that I'm an authority on the subject and they'll contact me and that's a better position for me to be in from a negotiation perspective and from a marketing perspective. If you've got clients coming to you then you don't have to spend as much on advertising.

How to Get Clients to Come to You

I started blogging on TypePad. The reason I chose TypePad was I looked around and Seth Godin uses TypePad and if it's good enough for Seth Godin, it's good enough for me.

Robert: And he's still there too.

Ryan: He's still there but I found out later that if he wished he would have done it on his own domain, rather than on TypePad.

Robert: And now it's too late?

Ryan: Yes, now it's way too late. I also did that for a couple of years and then I started thinking about getting my own domain because I thought I don't own typepad.com. I have to keep paying them a fee every year and if they ever decided to shut me down, I'm in a really vulnerable position. I ended calling up Ryan Healy in Seattle, he owned ryanhealy.com and I bought that domain from him for $160.

Robert: And you probably could have paid five or six grand?

Ryan: I don't know that I would have paid that much. I actually don't know how much I would have paid for it but at the time he hadn't done anything with it for a whole year and I thought I'll see if he's open to selling it and it turns out he was. I paid him for the site and I'm really glad I did because since then there have been other Ryan Healy's out there doing stuff online. I also registered with .net and .org, etc., and that's where I moved my blogs. I finally went to WordPress and I've been blogging there since January of 2008, a little over three years.

Robert: Now all these things work together?

Ryan: Yes, and last fall I started sending out a print newsletter to my clients as well as a few potential clients and once again it demonstrates authority, it stays in touch with clients so if they have copy needs they're going to pick up the phone and call me. Each newsletter has little ad blocks saying if you need help on this project pick up the phone and call me.

You've got to start somewhere but you probably don't want to stick just with the strategy you start with or the technique that you start with. I want to start to look at how I really build the business that starts to send potential clients to me on a regular basis without me having to go and chase clients.

Robert: You grow and you get bored with this one technique. What's funny is every now and then I have customers call Lance or I if we are having a promotion and that alone makes it worth it because they're interrupting your day and not vice versa.

Ryan: Right.

Robert: On the other hand, it would have been hard to start there?

Ryan: Yes. Nobody knew who Ryan Healy was in 2005.

Robert: But now you can say here's my sales letter, here's a testimonial from Alex Mandossian, or from Michel Fortin.

Ryan: Yes. Now I have the credibility, not as much as some people, some people have been in the business for two, three, four decades who are way beyond where I am but at least I can point to my site and tell them go to these testimonials. I also have a samples page where people can read my sales letters.

Robert: Yes, that's a better way to do it. It sounds as if we could put this into some sort of a system that people could follow. You started out, you went on to a job site and you found people who needed copy, you looked at local business flyers and then you called them on the phone. For a lot of people that's scary but you picked up the phone, figured out how their business was doing and then saw where the conversation went and turned it into how can we make this flyer or form letter convert better.

You got to that point and then you made a sales letter explaining what you do, showing testimonials but the call to action on this was for them to call you so that was another lead generation. Then you started going to seminars and by having a conversations and making friends you figured out who needed a copywriter, so that was another form of income. Then you started blogging and talking about this headline technique and that led to keywords from Google. You started doing AdWords and now you have a follow-up newsletter with the clients to keep them interested in you.

I've hired a couple of copywriters. They got the job done, and they were pretty good but I forgot about them. There was one person in particular that would email me once a month. She kept checking to see if I had any sales letters that need written, please keep me in mind and after six months she stopped and that was four or five years ago.

Recently she contacted me again and said she was in debt, she wasn't making any money and asked if I could put her on an autoresponder. I asked if she had a blog I could go to and see how she was as a person, it's not that much extra work, but it makes such a difference.

Ryan: Exactly. It makes a huge difference over time. In any service business, you have to stick around long enough for success to happen. If you're just going to try it out for a month or two what's the point?

Robert: You have to start somewhere too. I know some people would say I'm too good to fix up someone's flyer, I'm too good to get paid $200 for a job but that's $250 that you would have made in one or two days working in a regular job. Now you're working for yourself doing something you enjoy and you don't even have to leave home. You're getting paid a day's worth of work for an hour.

Ryan: Right. It's much better. I remember that specifically and I was so excited. I thought some people might make a lot more than that but at the same time I thought this was fantastic for me. It's so low risk and that was the big thing for me. This is something I can do and even with my lack of experience, I know I can do better and confidence is a big part of being successful.

Robert: All you're out is your time or maybe your dignity if someone hangs up on you but you didn't have to buy a Burger King or buy a Pizza Hut, you didn't have to go hundreds of thousands of dollars in debt, you just tried to get hired for this writing job.

Ryan: Trust me, it's way better to invest some sweat equity upfront and do some things like that to start a business than it is to invest in something like you were talking about. Before I ever became a freelance copywriter, I lost $30,000 on a vending machine business.

Robert: And then you started investing in yourself instead of vending machines and somehow it worked out?

Ryan: Yes.

Robert: We have a few minutes left, so let's discuss your newsletter, is it a print newsletter?

Ryan: Yes, it's a print newsletter.

Robert: Is there anything else you have in the works to take your copywriting and your freelancing to the next level?

Ryan: Right now, I'm really focused on creating products in various niches but I do have a report that I wrote about getting clients as a copywriter and I'm going to be rewriting that shortly. Later on, I'm going to be writing a course on how to succeed in the freelance business, not necessarily as a copywriter but focusing on all people who are in freelance businesses, web designers and copywriters. Those are two of the projects in the works right now.

Robert: Are you making these projects to get more leads for you or to get some extra income?

Ryan: Extra income. As far as the copywriting goes, lately I've had so many leads coming in that it comes to a point where saying yes to another job means I'm doing a disservice to the clients that have already hired me. I'm trying to focus on the clients I have at the moment. I have a couple of opportunities with clients where they're willing to pay me a percentage on performance in addition to the copywriting fee and so I'm moving more towards those types of arrangements. In six years of freelance copying I've been burned a lot, but really if, you can make the fee plus percentage work that's better than just a fee.

Robert: It sounds like fun.

Ryan: Yes, that's more the direction I'm going in because at that point you're sharing in the profit of the business and you're seen as more than just a copywriter even though you are a copywriter but...

Robert: You get paid better than one?

Ryan: Yes, you get paid better than one too. On the copywriting front that's the evolution of where I'm headed.

Robert: Sounds exciting. You'll be like one of those people who has had 40 years of copywriting in no time.

Ryan: I'll enjoy the moment and enjoy every day and see where it takes me.

Robert: It's all you can do. If my listeners want to find out more about you and what you do and how they can stay in touch, where should they go?

Ryan: The best place is my blog, ryanhealy.com. There are already 350 plus articles that I've written there. There's also a 'best of' tab so if you want to look at some of the better articles I've written, Evergreen Pepper stuff, you can click on that and thumb through those articles.

"Freelance Copywriting" with Ray Edwards

About Ray Edwards

Hi, my name is Ray Edwards (though you have probably already figured that out).

I'm probably best known as a Direct Response Copywriter, Internet Marketing Strategist and conference speaker.

I've had the good fortune to work with some stellar clients, including New York Times Best-selling authors Jack Canfield and Mark Victor Hansen (creators of Chicken Soup for the Soul), Joel Comm (author of Twitter Power and The AdSense

Code), Raymond Aaron (author of Double Your Income Doing What You Love) as well as Armand Morin, Alex Mandossian, Jeff Walker, and many others.

No matter what your business, chances are you need to: Attract new customers. Get your current customers to make bigger purchases, more often. Extend the life of a customer so they stay with you forever.

My specialty is helping you do all three of the above – faster, better, and with less human effort on your part.

Radio Disc Jockey Jumps Ship

Ray: I'm a person who, for 25 plus years, was in the radio broadcasting business. I was a disc jockey, and program director, and a station manager, and became a vice president for a radio company.

Around 1999-2000, I started to see the handwriting on the wall for the radio business and decided to transition into doing online marketing. The reason that it's so important to share with people is you are in the right place at the right time.

I was early because everybody thought I was crazy when I left a six-figure job with health benefits and everything that went along with it. I got to meet the stars and playing out backstage with concerts and all that kind of stuff. It was a lot of fun, but everybody thought I was crazy but I saw what was coming.

It's only just now began to be evident that the internet has changed everything. So, I became the copywriter of choice for a lot of well-known names in the marketing industry and some mainstream like Tony Robbins.

He's been my client on multiple occasions and the "Chicken Soup for the Soul" persons, and of course, the top names in the internet marketing like Armand Morin and Michel Fortin and Joel Comm, tons of people. Mainly, that happened for me because I was in the right place at the right time.

Also though, because I knew how to communicate effectively and persuasively mainly through writing, but it's so much more than that. People say we are copywriters. Aren't you bothered by things like video and audio and all that stuff?

No, it's all copy. So what makes me special is the same thing that can make anybody special, it is just knowing the techniques of communicating clearly and persuasively in this medium that we call the internet.

Robert: You said there are people who are worried fully, that things like video and WordPress are going to make you out of date, so you adapt just like you adapted to the internet in the first place, right?

Ray: Yes. Absolutely. If there's one continuum in my life, in my professional life, and in my life as a whole, I think it's communication. Think about this. Everything that we want in life is really leading us to an emotional state. We want money, or we want to get out of debt, or want to be in a better relationship, and we want all those things so we can feel happy.

The first communication that has to happen is communication with ourselves the possibility that that can really happen. Because its happened for other people, it can happen for me, too. It's communication. The second communication that we need with ourselves is there is a set of skills that allow some people to get more out of life and less of what they don't want. Again, those skills are communication.

I was in the communications business when I was in radio and I saw that the medium of choice, the method of distribution to the massive people was changing. It was no longer going to be radio. It was going to be the internet and through all kinds of technology that has changed.

When I first started, audio was just beginning. Broadcast dotcom was just beginning to be part of the internet and it was choppy audio. Everybody was throwing 56k motto. That's all changed now. Now, it's video. People have their own video channel on YouTube, but it's still all those communications.

Don't be worried for me as a copywriter because really, that's just one form of persuasive communication. That's what I really am trying to communicate to people now, Robert, is that if you can just communicate your message clearly and persuasively then you can get what you want out of life.

It's my belief that you want to do that the way it serves not just yourself but it serves other people, too, because that's the only way to be at it for a long time over a sustained period, it's really just about persuasive communication.

Robert: That makes sense to me. You said you were in the radio business. How did you even know that any of this goofy and crazy internet stuff existed?

Ray: It's pretty funny. I started to look for ways to increase our listenership at radio stations. I was in a programing side for a long time and wasn't involved in the sales side. But there are two things that I figured out. The people who drove the nice cars in the parking lot at the radio stations were not the DJs. They were the sales people. So, I decided to start making friends with the sales people. I also came from an entrepreneurial background.

My family were entrepreneurs. My grandfather owned two businesses. My mom owns several businesses. My dad owns his own business. I understood the dilemma of the small business owner because radio people, were trying to have small business owners do radio commercials and they were always schlepping the latest spot package.

I knew that those small business owners were not interested in packages and discounts. They were interested in their cash register. They're interested in people coming through their door and giving them the money. I studied how to write good ads and I discovered this person named Jay Abraham and I actually discovered him through a tape, it was a tape in the first edition of a Tony Robbins PowerTalk.

It was an interview that Tony did with Jay Abraham and Jay was just talking all about these genius ideas about how writing the right kind of copy direct response ads instead of what he called institutional advertising which is the kind that just talks about, "We've been around for 25 years serving our community over it."

That doesn't help anybody. But the kind of ads that worked were the ones everyone makes fun of like the Smokeless Ashtray, and Spray on Hair and all that kind of stuff because they actually asked you to place an order. I thought, "What a cool idea. We'll do that for our radio plans." So I became known as the person who wrote good ads for the clients.

Then, I started studying direct response advertising and copywriting and I thought, "Hey, we could use this to grow the listenership of the radio stations and promote our shows." I started doing all kinds of direct mail and direct response TV. If you think about it, if you've seen ads and asked for radio stations on television, it's usually a bunch of song clips.

I was the person who was running ads that said, "Listen tomorrow morning at 7:00 o'clock and win $10,000," because I thought, Well, I want them to listen. I don't care if they like the songs or not. I just want them to listen to radio station, so we'll bribe them. That was direct response.

Writing on the Wall

Then, I saw iPods and satellite radio coming down the pike and I thought, "You know what, it's going to be way easier for people to listen to the songs they want to listen to instead of listening to free over the air radio and radio is not going to respond to this and it's going to hurt the business and that's going to hurt the advertising business."

I just saw that everything that radio was doing that people were so enamored with was going to move to the internet. It doesn't mean that good radio operators can't still make money. They obviously can, but I have been studying direct response advertising all this time. I didn't know this in preparation for the ultimate direct response copywriting medium of all time and that is the internet.

Robert: Cool. Then, from there, you worked as a full time copywriter, right?

Ray: Yes. I made a deal with my wife. I said, "Look, I think I can make a go with this copywriting thing and here's the deal. When my copywriting income equals my radio salary, I'll quit the radio business." I was making a six-figure salary in radio. It sounded like a good plan until it actually happened. Then I realized, "Wow. If I can do this, I'm going to cut my pay in half," because I was making two 6-figure salaries.

One from my own business and one from my radio job. It took me a few months. I still hesitated even at that point, but on July 4 of 2006, I cut the cord and said goodbye to radio. That next month, my copywriting income doubled, and a couple of months later it tripled, and I never looked back.

Robert: Sure. So, problem's solved then?

Ray: Yes. The problem was nonexistent. It was only in my head.

Robert: Okay. At that point, you were taking on freelance jobs as a copywriter?

Ray: Yes. My first pay job was $400 for a sales letter and I was blown away because in the radio business, the DJs write the copy. Most people don't know that the DJs write the copy and they don't get paid anything to do it.

Think about what you're getting. If you're buying radio ads and you get this song and dance about how they're going to make you these great ads, some $10 DJ wrote your ad for free and hated doing it. I got paid $400 to write a sales letter and I thought that was awesome. Then, I wrote a sales letter for $750 for a person named Michael Litman who hired me off the Warrior Forum. Then, I found out that I was way undercharging. I found out that people were getting $3,000 to $5,000 for a sales letter but I still couldn't believe that.

I thought that's got to be made up. Litman emailed me real quick and said, "I need two more sales letters." I'm thinking, "Yes. Of course you do because I'm the cheapest copywriter on the planet." I called him up and I said, "Look, I hate to do this but I need to raise my rates."

I Just Cut My Fee in Half!

He taught me something in that moment. He said, "Wait. Stop talking and just tell me how much it is." I said, "Okay. It's $2,000." Now, I'm thinking a thousand a piece and he says, "Each?" "I mean, $2,000 for both of them." He says, "Each?" I didn't totally internalize the lesson. I said, "No, for both of them." "Okay, great. Done." But afterwards I realized, "Oh, he's going to pay me four grand and I just cut my fee in half."

My next job was $3,500 and then $5,000. It took me while till I got up to $7,500. I mentioned a couple of times that the problem is all on your head. Here's a real illustration of how that is so true. I was at about $ 7,500 in sales letter at one point. It was near Thanksgiving, and I got a phone call from a client who was recommended to me, sent to me by, Mike Feldstein who I'd written some copy for.

Feldstein said, "You should get this person to write your copy." I had decided by that time that I was going to take November and December off. I was going to do any copywriting. I just want to spend time with my family because I had never in my life been able to do that. I have the freedom to do this now and I was going to two months off. Who gets to take two months off?

I got a call and they tell me that they want me to write for this product launch that they're doing. I didn't want to take it but I didn't want to offend them, and I don't want to offend Mike. So, I thought I'll overprice myself to the point that they have to say no.

I listened to their whole spiel and finally they said, "How much would it cost you to do this whole project?" I said, "It would be $15,000." There's just a bit of silence, and they asked, "Okay. How do you want that? In a check or how am I going to pay you?"

I was in an alternate reality for a few seconds. I suddenly changed my whole thought process about not working for November and December and I said, "A check would be fine. You could write that to me," and we finalized the deal.

A similar thing happened to me when I raised my rate to $30,000. So if you're thinking about, "I want to write, or communicate, or turn what I know into money and I don't know what people are going to pay for it," here's what I've learned. They would pay you what you believe it's worth, not what they believe it's worth.

Robert: By that you mean even if you price it really high and you still, at some level didn't believe it, you're saying that it's not going to work? You have to actually believe that it's the timeout?

Ray: I think that that is true most of the time. I don't think it's a universal magical law but it's mostly true. It should go without saying you have to be able to live with the goods.

If your work isn't good, then it won't take long for the word to get around and nobody will pay you anything. So, that's got to be the gift that you're actually doing something that's worth money.

This is why writing sales copy, whether it's sales letters or video sales letter scripts or auto responders, it's the best-paid writing you can do because people who pay you to do it are paying for return-on-investment. They're buying dollars at a discount.

They figured, "Well, if I'm going to pay this person $30,000, I'm going to make $3,000,000 on his promotion, so that's a total win for me. I don't mind paying 30 grand if I think it's going to get $3,000,000."

Robert: What you mean by that is that if they're hiring you as a ghostwriter and they say, "Here's 20 grand to make me a book," then they can't measure that, but if they're writing a sale letter, they can say, "Okay. I gave this person 15 grand and I got a hundred, now I can really easily tell its worth versus what I paid it for.

Writing Riches

Ray: Yes. Being a ghostwriter is another word to get well-paid, but I think it's harder to get well-paid as a ghostwriter than it is as a sales writer because there's that immediate auto eye that the entrepreneur who will pay you can see and they're doing it because they believe that if they hire the right copywriter that will be the leverage they need to make more money. That's why they're willing to pay these insane amounts of money.

That's one of the reasons why I don't do a lot of writing copy for clients. I do a few clients every year because with the right client I love doing the work, and I enjoy the process, and I enjoy working with them while they're launching their product.

One of the things that happened for me was this very famous marketer called me up the following Christmas, and wanted me to write a copy for him for a launch he was doing over the Christmas holiday.

I tried to tell him, "I don't think that's a great idea," but he was determined to do it, because it's Christmas. Who's paying attention to internet marketing launches?

It turns out lots of people, but that's a different story. Anyway, he paid me 30 grand upfront and paid like a prince. But what happened was when I told him my price, I heard him tapping on a calculator at the other end of the phone and he said, "Okay. Let's see. If I pay you $30,000 with it, we're going to make X number of sales. It's going to be $3,000,000 revenue and we're going to come out." He's doing this whole calculation and he's just muttering all the numbers out loud. For the first time, I was slapped in the face and realized, "Oh. I think I'm doing great for getting paid 30 grand to write sales letter. Meanwhile, he's banking $3,000,000."

Robert: So he's got a huge discount from you and you didn't even realize it.

Ray: Yes. I realized, "I need to be selling my own stuff. I need to be the $3,000,000 person." That's been my focus mostly since then. For people who can pay my fee, now it's $50,000 plus a percentage. I'm trying to get a piece of the pie and I only work with clients that I think I'm interested in the project and I think he would be fun to work with.

But for anybody who's got these skills, this is one of the beauties of copywriting for me, Robert, is that anybody who wants to break into internet marketing, who's had trouble trying different systems and they couldn't make it work, they tried the magic speed bullet system it's, "I didn't make real money."

They still believe and know in their hearts that they can make a living, a good living. They can actually become wealthy on the internet but they don't know how, this is the greatest way, in my opinion, to do it. You don't even have to be great. You just need to be a competent copywriter.

You can get really well-paid, make more money than most people who work in jobs, have free time, make your own schedule, take your own vacations, work from anywhere in the world, you can do all that and get paid to learn about having a business online. Do you think that when I worked for Alex Mandossian, Jeff Walker, Rich Schefren, the StomperNet people, Andy Jenkins, Brad Feldman, Armand Morin, Tony Robbins, Mark Victor Hansen, and Jack Canfield, that I learned anything when I was working on those projects?

Robert: Tons every time, I'm sure.

Ray: Yes, because I got access, first of all, to whatever $2,000 or $5,000 or $10,000 training I've written a copy for. So that's the first level. The next level is I had behind-the-scenes view of how everything was happening for the promotion where I got to see the good, the bad, and the ugly, the stuff that works, the stuff that didn't work.

I got a paid education I never had to pay for, certainly better working conditions than most people, absolutely a better boss than most people because I was my own boss, and I got to learn all this stuff, plus I got to meet all these people. So, when I did my first internet marketing book launch, I had friends who had lists.

I always like, "How do get I a list? How do you get JB Partners?" I think one of the best ways is to be a service provider who stands out above other service providers. I've worked hard to do that as a copywriter and build a relationship with my clients so that when you get ready to do your own promotional thing, they'll click the same button for you. My first JV Partner who first sent an email was Jeff Walker.

You Don't Even Have to Ask and You Shall Receive

I didn't even ask him. I told him what I was working on and he said, "Would you like me to mail for that?" Because he knew me, because I've done work for him, because we had a relationship, and that's how you do it. I was like, "I have worked with you before and I've promoted your stuff before."

First of all, because you do really great stuff, everything you do is golden and you're the most productive person I think I know, and I know you, so I have no problem promoting your stuff. On the other hand, like just this morning, I got messages on Facebook, from people wanting me to promote their stuff. I don't know them. I've never met them. One of them told me, "I want to give you an opportunity to promote my $37 ClickMate product which launches tomorrow."

Robert: Okay. Hearing your whole story, hearing how all this had happened, it just sounds like you decided, "I'm going to provide this service," and in your case it was copywriting because you'd done it, you'd enjoyed it in the radio business, and you were just like, "All right. I'm going to write it on forum.

I'm going to make a sales letter for whoever will pay me. I'll price whatever I feel like I'm worth right now, because in your first job, you can price what you want and then increase it later. It just sounds like from networking, from getting yourself out there, from ruffles, from word-of-mouth, the jobs just became larger and larger.

Then, at that point, you just grew to where you can pick and choose who you wanted to work for because once you have your repeat clients, you can stick with these people. You kept increasing your prices. Now you can say from $400 starting to, what, $1,000, $5,000, $15,000, $30,000, plus fifteen percent."

It just sounds like whatever kind of writing anyone wants to get into, especially if it's copywriting, then just starting to form network and then build up bigger every time.

Ray: Yes. I learned a lot back then and now I say, "I should have done this differently." The biggest thing was I only had my own products from the beginning. That was a mistake that I made and now I would say, "Now that I know what I know, the advice I would give to people who would ask me, 'what would you advise me to do?" "Do the copywriting gig and get paid but start having your own stuff." It's all copywriting.

You know this Robert. The articles that you write and you distribute to article services, the blog post, the podcasts, the interviews, it's all copy. It's all persuasive communication. Once you know the principles of writing good copy, you get to the point where you subconsciously just embed stuff in everything you do.

You're not thinking about it for a while. It just comes naturally but you just know the points of effective communication that get your message across, that get people to take the action you want them to take.

Robert: So you're saying that even if you're writing a 10-page report, even though it's technically not a sales letter, you're going to be thinking, "Okay. I'm going to have some bullet points here. I'm going to have something to grab them till they read the rest of the pages. They'll turn the page, so they read page two until they get to the end because I got the interested."

Yes. It's like anything you write, it's like a goal they used for writing in school, just make some big paragraphs, and spill it five more pages. Once you make that switch, suddenly it's fun. Suddenly it's like, "I'm getting fun from my readers." It's a whole different way of look at it.

Robert: Absolutely. Think about Tony Robbins as an example. He's written a book called "Awaking the Giant Within." It's a great book. Here's what most people probably don't realized. Most of the stuff that he teaches at his $5,000 and $10,000 weekends and weeklong seminars is in that book.

What is the book? It's really a form of sales copy for his live events. His whole deal is, "Look, I'll sell you a cheap book to get you interested enough to buy my $200, $300 or $500 audio or video program and I'll sell you the book to get you motivated to come to a live event."

I think the starting price for a live event for him is $800. That's the beginning level. So, you get there. What happens? You get immersed more into the experience and he sells you a $5,000 weekend or $60,000 platinum coaching program and it's all good.

I'm not saying that that's bad. It's just that it's strategically thought out. There's a reason for doing it. I'm sure when you're looking at a book project that way instead of just counting on, "I'm going to become a million selling author," but you think, "This is going to lead people into my world where I have all these other stuff to offer them," it becomes a lot different.

Like you said, it becomes a lot more fun to write the book, or write the article, or write the 10-page report. You're not going to start with a book. You can start with a 400-word article or a bunch of 400-word articles. I know you've got great systems for doing that. If they're now doing it, that's good because that's where it all begins.

Robert: All right. Sounds good to me. So, we're just about out of time and I understand that you have an awesome program for doing what we talked about today. We're infusing copywriting wherever it needs to go and make your writing it a durable process, making it easy, making it fast and getting paid for any kind of writing, right?

Ray: Yes. I've got a book that I wrote called "Writing Riches" and I created a membership community, which I know is something that you've been recommending.

In that membership community, I teach you all these different ways of applying the principles of persuasive communication of whatever you're writing. We're a good a community, and we have a forum. Every month I do website critiques where we get on our webinar and we look at people's websites with members of the community and I critique and give them suggestions, telling them what to take away, what put in, and what they might want to change.

Then once a month, we do a Q&A call or it's just open forums and you can just ask me anything that you want to ask. People pay me thousands of dollars for consulting. If you're consulting client, it's $10,000 a month minimal. That's the real numbers, not just something I made up. As part of being in this community, this is part of the deal. We have tutorials and then I just started a program that you'll get when you become a member of the community.

It's called "Writing Information and Sales." It covers how to apply, every kind of writing that you do as we cover everything from short reports, to ebooks, to doing teleseminars, to doing webinars, to doing sales videos, to doing sales pages, to freelancing for money, and we do it module by module, video step-by-step. I'll show you exactly how to do it.

"Speaking from the Stage" with David Cavanagh

About David Cavanagh

Hi, my name is David Cavanagh, a marketing "guru" who has coached hundreds of ordinary people just like you from "newbie marketer" to "marketing expert" with millions in the bank to show for it.

Needless to say that today, my life is exactly how I envisioned it to be.

I'm my own boss. I love what I do. I have time for myself and my family, and I'm stress and debt-free. (But don't get me wrong, it wasn't always this way).

In fact, when I first started out in marketing years ago, I was an unemployed single father living in Australia, who struggled to make a sale. My experience was so disheartening that I almost called it quits, so I know how you might feel right now because I've been there. And not that long ago either!

But something changed once I decided to motivate myself and kept in my mind that nothing would keep me from failing. I coached myself to success and soon afterward, I started coaching others - and today I want to coach you!

David will tell you that he was born into a working class family and had to earn every penny/cent that came his way. He needed to rapidly become street wise and a good communicator, especially when his skills didn't closely match the school curriculum!

Prior to earning and receiving international recognition and acclaim for his Best Internet Coaching Program for Newbies and founding The Cavanagh Success Academy, David worked many different jobs, including serving as a disk jockey, and studied widely including NLP and hypnosis. He has appeared on stage around the world as a guest speaker and trainer with some of the biggest names in NLP, Internet marketing and Business Training. He is now at a stage in his international career and reputation where he can invite international speakers and personalities such as Pat Mesiti to be guest speakers at some of the Cavanagh Success Academy workshops.

Profiting from Ugly Websites

David: Here's how I started making money online. First of all, I was on the Gold Coast in Australia, which is in Queensland in Surface Paradise and I moved to Broad Beach. I decided one day after talking to a few friends, that the internet looks all right. One of the people said to me, "Do you have a website?" I'm thinking a website, what's that? No, seriously one of the people said "Do you want a website?" I said, "Well what do I need a website for?" They saw I was DJing at the moment and I thought "What could a website have to do with a DJ?" And I honestly didn't have a clue what websites were.

I started going into to the local internet cafe and checking things out and thought this is pretty cool. I rang up one of my friends and asked him who did his website, and he told me that he did his own. I said, "Well I wouldn't mind learning how to actually create one and make some cash out of it. Because like you, I am an entrepreneur and I would like to know how you actually do those things." He said that he used Microsoft Front Page.

I asked him what to do. And he coached me on how to create the website. I started learning how to do it, and I convinced a few people in Broad Beach that they needed David Cabinets to design websites, and get them into Google and Yahoo and all that research engine optimization. I looked on the internet for BroadBeachGulfCoast.com because Broad Beach was the suburb, Gold Coast was the area, and it was available, so I created the website. Then one of my friends rang me and asked if I knew the owner of Beach Gold Coast tourism? I told him no and let me know that she would like to buy the domain name So, I was sitting there thinking really? I paid about $17 for it at the time and I went into a meeting with them and they paid me $8,000 for the domain name.

I just started with web design and like you, I had that tenacity to just go out there and I didn't take no for an answer.

Robert: Right, and that's huge and you and I tell people all the time that you just have to have something out there. If you just have an idea or you have a dream that doesn't really mean anything, no one is going to buy your dream for $8,000 but on the other hand if you happen to have that domain, right place right time then someone will pay for it.

Just Do Something!

David: Yes definitely. I know there are people out there who do affiliate marketing, some do local business, their own products and services, or private label. You know what, I don't disagree with anyone because everyone has got their own opinion but what I say to people is just go out there and do something and make some money out of it. Because most people sit there procrastinating and they never actually do anything, so just get out there and do something.

Robert: Right, and as long as you have something out there, and maybe if you are not making any money usually it's just a few things. If you have an opt-in page, a sales letter then you can change the offer, you can change the headline then it's these little baby steps. They don't have to set up this huge website.

David: It's like what you tell your students, it's just sometimes the little minor tweaks are what is going to take you from zero to hero. The thing is whether you are doing a corporate site, a mum and pop kind of website, or a local business site - as you said, they still have a headline, graphics, and text, which you and I know is copy on the page. Whether it looks like corporate design, or like a David Cavanagh/Roger Plank kind of marketing design, whatever - look at the client, look what they want, give the client what they want and take what you want - the dollars.

Robert: I love how you got started out not by making some big huge site that is going to change the world. You started by doing web design for individual people.

David: You should have seen the designs Robert, honestly they were disgusting. I had dolphins jumping all over the place and I had these marketing headlines going backwards and forwards, and the clients actually told me that it looked good. I look back at it now and think oh my gosh, I am not even going to put my name to that. Except if you go to I-Card.org you will see them and you will kill yourself laughing. But at the time, I who sold them to my clients. And the website was secondary to that, because they had a problem I gave them a solution and the solution was that they are in the top ten in Google under several hundreds of key phrases.

People always say keywords, I'd rather call them key phrases, they were in the search engines under multiple key phrases and they were getting hits to their sites, not just any hits but targeted hits, and we were capturing names and details. People were getting their info from the search engines and calling them up and closing deals. The website owner told me that it might be not much of a website but they were closing deals and putting money in the bank to keep it going.

Robert: Right, why mess with it.

David: And I didn't know what I was doing.

Robert: It didn't matter it was still making money, so you had this ugly website but you were getting paid for it and you set it up the proper way so that your clients were making money every day from it. I am sure there was tons of competition that had a perfect looking website that was not top ten in Google or was not even finished.

David: You better believe it. There were heaps of them out there, when I looked at some of them, I thought look at the piece of rubbish I've got and look how glamorous and sexy theirs are, and yet realistically mine got the hits. That's why when I look at the paper templates that you show your students, you probably get students saying that's only basic. But I think to myself yes, it's basic compared to what, and is doing the job, is it getting the point across and is converting

Robert: Right. It's funny because back when you were getting started there were so many of the flash intros, and the splash page and all kinds of music and animations, and today the equivalent of that are all these fancy WordPress sites. You see they have all these tabs and it says, there is this big orange button that says download here or opt-in here, and it looks good but everyone I know who has one of those fancy look sites, it converts but not as well as these direct response sales letters that look ugly but make more money.

David: I agree with you, because I think to myself basically people on the internet are buying one thing - a solution to a problem, and if you can solve the problem in a cost-effective way with the best service and the best support they don't really care half the time if the website hasn't got a sexy little thing on the side and a big banner sitting across the top as long as it gets the point across, it solves the problem and they've got somebody they can deal with.

Robert: And not only just convince me you can solve the problem, but if I can figure out how to buy the thing then, that is great.

David: I was in London the other day doing a seminar and I actually went to one page, it was through one of the Warrior Forum specials, and I thought this looks all right, I got to the person's page and it was awesome. It was a WordPress plug in and I looked at it and thought this looks really good, but there wasn't a buy button on the page.

Robert: Yep.

David: And I am thinking, I was sitting there, cash in my hand - ready to buy, and, some people put so much time and effort into their copy, into their headline and the layout and the fancy sexy buttons and they forget to put the most important thing on which is buy now or opt-in.

Robert: It's funny because even if all you had was a headline and a couple of bullet points and a buy button, that's better than the most beautiful, the most descriptive sales letter ever with no buy button.

David: Well I agree with you, and it's like I have seen some of your stuff you have put out there with the headline, bullet points, opt-in, etc., and I know they convert because you have shown me. And yet, I have seen these really-really long sales letters and people say they are too long. To me, there is no such thing as long sales letters but there are such things as boring sales letters. Copy to me, and words on a page should be like a ladies skirt. They should be long enough to cover everything but short enough to be revealing. You have to figure out, how long should it be, how short should it be, what's my point and am I solving the problem and is there a call to action? Go to the bottom of the page and put in your name, fill in this, buy now. You have to do it or you are going to miss out.

Robert: And you have to have something up there to adjust it, you can't adjust it in there, right?

David: Definitely not, you have to.

Bribe the Promoters!

Robert: So how in the heck can you get from being a web designer to being this person who speaks on all these stages around the world?

David: I bribe the promoters.

Robert: In what way?

David: No I'm just joking.

Robert: Knowing you I would have believed it.

David: I was working with Peter's son, marketing in Australia. Peter is a big marketer in Australia and all over the world, I was working for him doing copywriting and I talked to Brett McFall one day and I didn't know but Brett was about to start the World Internet Summit which had Ed Suber and Tom Huwa. Anyway I was on the phone with Brett and he said I have done this copy net, what do you think of it. Brett is like a leading copywriter, and I said well I don't know I don't think it is very good.

He came to see me and he had spent thousands and thousands of dollars in copy and his copy was bad, and when I look back at it, it was just my ego talking. I had put out a little script that I got someone to write for me called Number One Position, which helped people get into the search engines by having different key phrases all over the place.

I showed Brett that and he said that works really-really well, and I kept on begging him to show this at his upcoming World Internet Summit. He told me no that he had Armand Morin, and all these people from overseas. I asked him to give me a break, let me do something. He told me no again. That he had all these people from America and we don't need you. I said "No you do need me, that's the thing." I must have told him a hundred times, so he finally gave me a 30 minute guest spot in the lunch break, I ended up going for about 50 minutes.

I sold nearly all the crowd, and I think it was my nervous enthusiasm that got me over the line. And then he said, "We had so many people talking to us about you. We'd like to invite you to Nashville, Tennessee to talk."

At the time the only thing I could think of was the cost of the airplane fare. Brett assured me that he could help me out with that. It just went from there and I got on stage with people like Armand Morin, Ted Sebure and Paul Collig.

I went from the web designer who was basically out of work to the person touring the world teaching people, and don't get me wrong - when you are on those big stages as you know, you really have to start researching big time, finding out people's problems, getting the solution or otherwise the promoters get someone to replace you.

Robert: Right, and that is something that you keep mentioning on this call, it's all about helping people and finding their solution. And I can't tell you how many sales letters or products I see where someone says, hey look at this WordPress plug in I got, or look at this SEO I got, and I say well that's nice but it doesn't excite me, it doesn't get me to the top ten in Google. Or it doesn't get me all this extra traffic, so solve my problem and I will pay attention.

David: You are looking for the wow, you are looking for the why do I need it, what's in it for me and the person just hasn't convinced you because it's a nice sales letter but that's about it. They haven't sold you on why it solves your problem.

Robert: A lot of them are just too close to the product, and you made a good point with the nervous enthusiasm, it's like you need both. You need to see it from their point of view just to know that you are on the right track, but also you need to have an ego because otherwise you will never go on stage.

David: That's true, well it's like you when you came to Thailand and you spoke. I was thinking Robert's young, wonder how it will go, because I know he's all smart on webinars, but when you get in front of the audience you are a natural - you and Lance are both natural. Because you have talked to so many people each and every day, have done hundreds of webinars we all seem to be encountering that everyone has the same wants, desires, needs, etc.

Robert: I am still not moving as fast as I want to go, but that's a good point. Sure it might be scary to speak on stage, then run some webinars, teach a small group of people and just get your subject really down so that when it comes time to – present to the World Internet Summit or some other event, that way you are having fun.

How to "Become" Smart

David: You know what made me really smart when it comes to answering questions? Sometimes we that's a stupid question and yet that stupid question might be asked ten times by different people, and after a while you think if it's said once it's stupid but if it's said ten times, well it's not stupid and I have to include it in my course.

I know that I am a lot smarter than a lot of people that get on stage or do coaching because my students have given me the ammunition to be able to go out there and help others. I know that with you and Lance, because I see the same kind of thing... what you need, who are you targeting, what's the problem, how are you going to solve it, what's your headline, and what's your call to action.

You are doing exactly the same thing and yet I see people starting each and every day and I am frustrated because I think to myself, it's a proven formula. You solve a problem, you give them what they want in a way that's unbelievably affordable, best back up support and yet they are not doing it.

Robert: Why not?

David: Probably because they are stupid, but it's really good for you and me, because we can get more sales.

Robert: And that is such a good point, because I have seen people like Armand take out a flip chart and say - go one person at a time and say, "Ask me a question" and he will write down 20 or 30 questions. Like what's an opt-in page, how do I choose my keywords for Google, and at first when I saw that I was thinking how does Armand not pull his hair out by hearing all these newbie questions, but your biggest crowd is your newbies. No matter what niche it is, whether it's internet marketing or it's golfing or it's self-help or whatever - the newbie questions, are going to create your stage presentation.

David: John Childers said there is one thing, no matter what industry, no matter what niche, what's the hardest thing? And I am sitting there thinking I don't know. You know what it is - it's getting started, and that is where we really push to people who are getting started so we can help solve their problem. I think if we can solve problems, if we can help people, and if we can help them in a way that they really truly know they need us. Then we've done our job.

Robert: It really can be that simple, right?

David: When I first started it was ego and I thought I knew everything, and the thing is anyone listening to this call today or tonight, I think to myself drop your ego - your ego isn't your amigo. What you have to do is ask a question, shut up, listen and truly listen with two ears and one mouth and if you don't know the answer, go and find it out, solve it and put it into your database or your frequently asked questions.

Another thing that you and I shared ages ago, when people are writing their sales page on the left hand side of the page, and then on the right hand side I will solve them. I will put it together and instead of calling it a frequently asked questions page, I will have it as my sales page, because all a smoke screen, the objections, every single thing is actually put together on that page. And if I get anymore through my support desk, I will add them as well.

Robert: Right. And that is really cool because that just comes down to know which questions I am going to ask first to make it all float. Your customers or your future customers have already most of your sales copy for you.

David: Exactly, and I noticed that when you did a lot of your Speed Copy, the same kinds of things. Robert might present different to David, and David might be different to Lance, etc., but at the end of the day if it's working. If people are making money, solving people's problems, helping, etc., the bottom line is if the job is getting done and people are all happy and smiling and putting money in the bank, well we have all done our job.

Robert: I can't put it any better myself. I guess for anyone listening to this - you can have an ugly site, and if you have a site that looks like crap but actually collects opt-ins or actually has a buy button or gets sales, then that's something to start with. And you can improve it, and as long as it makes money, who really cares right. What David did was he started out by just getting paid for doing something and by solving somebody's problem and just repeating that.

He got started with doing web design and did all kinds of stuff, and eventually got to the point where he had a piece of software, but his problem was that not enough people were able to look at this software, so he went out and spoke to one person and did his best to get himself on stage. Almost didn't make it, but he was actually able to get in front of the stage of all these people, demoed his software - and one thing led to another.

I think people out there, as long as you are figuring out what people need to get started, no matter what niche you are in - what are their problems, what are their questions, what kinds of things keep coming up over and over again, that's what your product should be about. Whether it's a membership site, a book or a piece of software, and that is what you should use to write your sales letters.

I think that's really what it all comes down to, if you think of a bunch of stuff to throw at people, that is not necessarily what is going to be what they need. But as long as you are answering their questions, if one person has this question you can pretty much bet that other people have the same question and the internet is big. But it's also kind of small right, because people can't easily find the solution to how do I get a domain name, how do I get a website. You need to make something that you can pass around over and over.

You could just make a product or have some kind of a coaching program where you can say, here you go, here's how to do it. David - if people want to know more about what you are up to, what you are doing, where should they go?

David: The best thing for them to go to is GettingStartedOnTheInternet.com. Or they can go to DavidCavanagh.com and I am starting up a brand new site in about two weeks, which is going to be the best coaching program. And by all means I would love to get your people onto a call with you, and I will even give them a special discount just to help them out, because anyone who is a friend of yours and Lance's is a friend of ours. I will be more than happy to share anything.

Robert: All right, perfect let's do it and the same to you - so that is DavidCavanagh.com and then a little easier to spell GettingStartedOnTheInternet.com. Thanks for being here David.

David: And thank you very much for having me, and I look forward to helping you and any of your students with any questions or answers they want. Thanks very much for having me aboard.

"Software, Seminars, and Memberships" with Armand Morin

About Armand Morin

If you've been on the Internet at all over the past 15 years, you have seen Armand Morin whether you knew it or not. Either by seeing the end result of one of his many products, one of his student's websites, or by simply seeing his name on hundreds of thousands of websites all over the Internet.

Armand Morin, self-made multimillionaire, author, and best-selling recording artist, is one of the most well-known Internet marketers in the world today. Having started online in 1996, his personal businesses alone have generated over $80,000,000 in revenue.

Armand has taught tens of thousands of people from all walks of life in 101 different countries his amazingly unique and proprietary Internet business building principles and strategies, as well as his unconventional, no-nonsense life design and management skills.

Armand is known for revealing his latest epiphanies, his wildly successful, no-nonsense strategies, and his proven marketing models that are profitable, ethical, and ignored by 99% of the marketing world.

Selling Software without Knowing a Single Line of Code

Armand: My business is divided into two different things. Number one is teaching people how to market their businesses online, and number two I would actually say that my business is simply the same thing, which is product development. Meaning, finding products that people actually want, and developing them either through our own team or having somebody else develop them for us, or developing a course to teach something that someone wants to know.

Robert: Software and courses?

Armand: Yes, pretty much.

Robert: I think the first way I heard of you was you had a piece of software called E-Book Generator.

Armand: Yes.

Robert: Can you tell us a little bit about how that came to be, and about all that software you ended up making?

Armand: Yes absolutely. E-Book software is actually the very first software that I actually created. I don't even know what the date was, but it was a long time ago. I was going to create an E-Book, in fact there was a book that I had for many years, and I think I had it for about 8 years called Take Online Payments. What had just happened, just to kind of give you a little bit of background, is that I had my Merchant Account taken away from me. We had this big launch, when I first got started in the world of Internet Marketing where we made $4.2 million over the course of 12 weeks. This was at the time when no one has ever thought of actually doing something like that. They pulled my Merchant Account away.

I was stuck without a Merchant Account. Now at that point I had proven to myself that the internet worked, so I decided to figure out a way to process credit cards online without a Merchant Account, and I discovered something called third party payment processors, which most people would think of as PayPal or 2CheckOut, or AlertPay, or ClickBank. Those are the most popular ones today. But at that time, no one had ever heard of any of these companies, and I discovered there are a lot more. There are actually, over 80 companies, and so I took this information and found that a lot of people were searching for this too, so I decided to write an E-Book.

The problem was, in order to write an E-Book I needed some kind of software to compile this E-Book together. And at the time, PDFs weren't really the main type of E-Book out there. There was basically what is called E-Book software, which would take a web page and compile a bunch of web pages together into a single EXE file, like a software file, and it would have its own browser where you could scroll through the web page, and that is what the software does.

In this process, I bought the first E-Book software and it did almost everything I wanted it to do. Then I bought the second E-Book software and it also did most of what I wanted. I probably bought about six or seven E-Book software before I realized that none of them did what I wanted them to do. So I had this idea, if someone actually created a software that had all the good things that I needed, and none of the bad things that I saw on all this other software, they could probably make a lot of money. And then the second thought came up, why can't I develop that software? The problem was, was that I didn't know how to make software.

I remember someone telling me, "If you don't know how to do something then pay someone else to do it." Very simple phrase, but I think it is very applicable today as it was even back then. I found this company, in Czechoslovakia and I hired them, I paid them a lot of money. In fact, that one software is the most money I ever spent on a piece of software. I spent $5,000 initially in order to develop that. I had them develop it, I put it out there on the market and that is how we developed our first software.

But that software was not the most amount of money I spent on that software. Over the years, I have probably spent - I will say $75,000 in total.

Robert: Just improving it?

Armand: Yes, improving it and getting features that people wanted. The important thing about that is many of these features that people wanted weren't features that I actually thought were necessary. They were actually what my customers wanted. So if I thought it would enhance the software and give people more options then I added that feature. I think a lot of people, when they are developing things or doing things, try to please absolutely everybody when there is no way you can actually do that. We try to go with what the masses want and then once we have a feature and we have tested it and worked it through, then we release the product out in the marketplace.

That was how we developed our first software. Then people started asking us questions, "How do you create that header graphic that you have on your website?" So we created a software that essentially made it easier for people to create a graphic for the top of their website. And then people were asking me, "How do you make that graphic book cover?" And so we created a term, named E-Cover.

The only problem was I couldn't think of what to name the software so I called it E-Cover Generator. All my software took on the last part of Generator. We named them all the same thing in order to create a product line, rather than just a single product. I think that is really important for people to understand, is that even though I happened into creating a series of products, most people today should really go into business with that thought. How do my other products actually fit, how do my new products fit in with my existing products, and are these the logical progression that my customers would actually want or need.

Robert: That makes sense, and it's kind of funny how you were talking about you invented the term E-Cover, because I remember you also had Pop-Over Generator.

Armand: That is an interesting because that Pop-Over Generator which created kind of like a pop-up that really wasn't a pop-up on a website, actually came from the results of a conversation with John Reese on the phone late one night. And John actually came up with the term Pop-Over.

Robert: Yes, I remember there was a pop-up and there was a pop-under but no one had a pop-over and there was yours. Everyone else who tries to compete with you is screwed because you were first and they are comparing themselves to you.

Armand: Exactly.

Robert: So that's pretty cool, and I always liked how a lot of people always think that maybe they can't make a training course, or they can't make software. Most training out there, most software looks like people just made stuff up, like a programmer just said, "Whatever. I am going to make an E-Book software" and they don't actually use it.

You had a unique insight on that because you actually had to make an E-Book software and had to improve it, paying the extra money to get the extra features added. Other people were using it and making it better for you. At the same time, you weren't making it overly complicated. It's like WordPress for Joomla, it gets too techy. WordPress is really simple. It's like an Apple product almost. Joomla can do all kinds of crazy stuff, but no one can use it.

Armand: When it comes to software, especially some of our early software, the basic premise for making it easy to use was we tried to look at and make the software work with the least number of clicks. That was the whole goal. Is this click necessary, can we remove it, can we make it easier for a person to use? And so the simplicity, we always tried to focus on, in order to do that. I think a lot of times today, in some of the things we are building, it's always about simplicity and how do we get people to really pay attention and actually use the software.

If they don't use the software, they are not going to buy anything else from us. Or if they listen to one of our courses, if I make it sound too complicated, and I don't show them exactly how to do it, they are not going to buy another product from us. And so our whole goal is to not only get that one sale, but also to get people to buy additional products from us because our products were so good. They are happy.

Robert: Yes, and it's like when there's that next product, they are buying it somewhat based on what it is, but also based a lot on who you are, because they trust you.

Armand: Right, the previous experience with us that is exactly what we are focusing on.

Robert: Right, and so speaking of making things simple and reducing the number of clicks. I have noticed that's a lot of how you do your marketing and how you give advice because I have had people give me advice, or explain a concept to me and we will draw this huge diagram with all these boxes and arrows, a Mind Map. Then when I asked you for advice, you will just say all right, just do this, make this web page, make this video, do this training course and that's it. And then you can improve from there. I really like that, keeping it simple and not getting in your own way I guess.

Armand: I think a lot of times that you have to go through this long explanation because they don't know what they what or what they actually need. And if I'm giving advice to you, you know my ultimate question is what do you want? And even if I don't ask, I know what you want, so my advice really is the shortest point to actually get what you want from that question - does that make sense?

Robert: It makes sense to me. Good stuff, and when you were marketing things like E-Book Generator or like Flash Generator, you had all of these competitors who were more complicated and they sold themselves more on features. How do you compete with that? Because you can say I'm simpler, but then they say I'm going to do a comparison, and I have a bunch of stuff Armand doesn't.

Armand: There are two strategies to it; number one is to market first, I think that is one of the main things, I think in almost any product category you are going to have other people come behind you. I read an article one time, it was about companies that were the first to market, and the example that they gave was aspirin. The company that first came out with aspirin, all they did was just sell aspirin. And then other people came out and they sold aspirin after that. But they showed the studies as far as market share after a period of time.

That first company that came to market still owned 67% of that market share, which was very interesting. Now I don't know if that necessarily relates on all categories, but I think it probably has a pretty good estimate as far as what happens when you are talking about market share, if a product is obviously promoted properly. So it's first to market, ease of use and then if anything I would say great support on the back end.

Robert: All right, first to market, ease of use, great support - that's pretty simple. One thing I really want to kind of find out about is this whole seminar thing. You ran like this huge seminar for seven years. How did you even think to do that?

The Largest Internet Marketing Seminar in America

Armand: Actually in the beginning it was an idea of a friend of mine, and he said well why don't we do a seminar? The whole story is that we launched the seminar, but the first big seminar was a complete flop. We actually never did it. Here's why, we put my friend's name at the top of it and I helped him market it. So the first seminar, we only had 20 or 30 people showing up. I decided to cancel it because I can't have speakers flying in to talk to only 20 or 30 people, because it was really my reputation on the line with these other people, and because they were all friends of mine.

We canceled it, and we relaunched it about six months later and we put my name at the top of it, and that was actually the first big seminar, in January of 2003.

We did it in Dallas, Texas and we had about 161 people there, and the whole concept was I had been to other seminars, I had seen what they were doing and I knew that we could certainly do them better by just providing little things they didn't or providing better training. Because many of these training seminars that I went to, were very unorganized. Even to this day, when I go to a seminar it shocks me how unorganized the seminar is. I have to give people a little bit of leeway because there is a lot to do in a seminar, but if you are going to have people pay you in order to attend an event you have to have great training and more importantly, we built a big seminar and it was a great experience from the moment that they walked in.

That is why we did things other people didn't do, such as feeding everybody, we paid for lunches every day and we had a big dinner on Saturday night. But at the same time the experience that they walked away from, just from feeding them, was probably as much if not more important than the actual training that they had, because they were allowed to network more and they could have a great networking experience.

Robert: Makes sense to me. Why are you not doing it anymore?

Armand: There are just so many things I think the seminar business is changing quite dramatically. I knew that it was really time to move on, we were doing other things, and my interest had changed. It's difficult dealing with nine or ten speakers, at that time we were doing them twice a year then we dropped down to only once a year. But doing my own trainings is a lot easier for me, because I just have to show up. And our team has done seminars so much that we can really put it together with our eyes closed, as far as putting on the seminar and handling the whole experience. And even now, because we are reinventing ourselves in the seminar business, is that we are still making tweaks and modifications in order to even make that better

At the end of every event, everyone is leaving and getting ready to go home. I have my whole team that were at the seminar come up to my room and then we sit down and we go through, literally every aspect of the seminar to see what people got, what people didn't get, is there anything that we missed, can we do this differently, how should we do it better next time? So we have this breakdown of the whole event after the fact in order to improve ourselves going forward. Even from the marketing aspect of it.

We are already planning what the next event is, but more importantly the marketing of that event. Because you don't have the credibility of nine or ten other speakers to get people to come, there is only me. What we have to do is say what are these people going to get and how are they going to get it. So we need to think about the marketing strategy, the positioning of it and then obviously the carrying it through to the actual seminar and the actual event. The other aspect that we have added recently was the live-streaming of the event, which we realized that we can get as many people that are in the room actually on the live-streaming.

That doubles our audience that we are speaking to, so if there are maybe 150 or 200 people in the room, we can have at least that many people online streaming and watching it from home. So we are still talking to a room of 300 or 400 people.

Robert: It's kind of cool how it all ties together, even the reason why you made this E-Book software, the reason why you did the seminar is that you see how either people are doing things wrong or how even you could be better, and that's why you are always changing based on what people want.

Armand: Yes, we are always trying to stay ahead of the market, what the market wants, what the market needs. Let me give you an example of that, I was doing some advertising on Facebook and there is a couple new strategies that I am implementing and one of them was basically to create a graphic and put it up on Facebook. The question I had was how could I make this easier for people to create a graphic without creating actual graphic software?

Robert: I was going to say make a Facebook graphic generator.

Armand: Yes, that's what we could do, but I said well what if I could do it a little bit different of a way. Basically I found an online software that works through your browser that's free, and then it allowed you to save an actual file. What I am going to do is I am going to use this online graphics program that's free, and create the graphics, the basic templates, that you can save as a proprietary format for that software. When I create this course and this video training on how I do this, a person will get these templates that they can upload into this free online software, and then from there they will be able to just replicate and follow me along on the course and create their own graphics the way they want. I will just make it very simple.

Robert: I wonder if you could even buy the rights and put it right there in the membership site.

Armand: Yeah, that probably wouldn't work with this particular company.

AM2 Mastermind

Robert: Oh darn. So close. Speaking of your training and your membership sites, whenever there is a big seminar, I always see you promoting your mastermind called AM2, so how did you get started with that?

Armand: AM2 started off as an idea. In fact the real idea behind AM2 is that a friend of mine, Alex Mandossian, came up with this idea to put together this training. In the first rendition of AM2 was actually, nothing like it is today. We actually had 12 people to begin with and the idea behind it was we will train you and in the back end you will pay us 5% of what your business does. That was the original agreement.

What happened was that worked to a certain degree, but we were always making improvements to it where we did trainings and brought other people in on our trainings, and it got to the point where Alex and I were going in two different directions. So when the opportunity came and Alex wanted to bow out of it, I bought him out and I took it over. Then we made some drastic changes and crated mini Master Mind groups.

This is the interesting part, because with AM2 we had these little tiny Master Mind groups where each one of my Platinum members would actually take over a Master Mind group. And, then they would do a once a week training. Well I thought that's what people wanted because that's what they said that they wanted, but what we discovered was because people were being held accountable each week, they didn't show up.

I decided to change this around, so we went to an online forum and we made some modifications, and that's worked out well as far as what we've been doing. Now there is even another step behind this that we have been working on for a long time, probably longer than what we should but it is to create our own social networking platform just specifically for AM2 where it works very similar to a Facebook, but it is just AM2 members participating in it. That's the next step for us.

But the idea behind AM2 really is to just give people the training and the up-to-date training not only weekly, but as the latest things that I may be working on coming up. For example, some of the new Facebook stuff that I am working on or some of the new things I am doing inside of WordPress. We run everything off WordPress, and we have done some things that other people haven't done yet. It's just to give them the training that they need in order to build their business and go forward, a new advertising strategy that I am looking at or new ways that we are looking at how we convert on our websites in order to make it better for us.

What I do is I look at myself as the guinea pig, where I will go first, I will either spend a bunch of money and try it out and if it works then I will be able to report back as far as how it works. If it didn't work then I will be able to say well this didn't work or that didn't work. They are not just getting a bunch of theory. Everyone is getting actually real world advice from someone who is actually doing it. I will show you my results and that's why if you look at almost any course I have ever done, I am always the example.

I will show you, this is what I did, this is my results and here's how you can do it too. And that is really the formula for every single one of my courses. I am talking about here's what I did using this technique and here's my results, and this is exactly how I did it and then I just walk people through step by step of what I just did.

Like you said earlier, where people may be thinking that they can't create a course, that's the process. You do it first, you prove that it works, so you may have a theory at first then you prove that it works, so it's no longer a theory it's an actual technique or strategy. And then you just simply go back and you explain to people exactly what you did in order to get those results. I think it's pretty easy.

Robert: That was one of the most important things I learned from you. Number one was double your prices, but number two was just do it, it's like just do what you were going to do anyway. If you were going to mess around with Facebook, then get the hang of it but then do it in front of someone, and I think that is a big difference than what you see a lot of marketers, especially new marketers do. I will see them just buy five courses on Facebook and then put them all together and then it's going in five different directions, it's super complicated.

But then the way I see you do things is first of you will say, I am going to give you everything you need, so if there is any kind of software templates, it's in there, but it's then it's something that you are going to do anyway.

Armand: When I look at my advertising strategies or anything that I am doing. I am look at it and at the same time in the back of my mind I am thinking, well I can do this but can other people do this? I am always thinking, this isn't just me doing a technique, it's actually market research. It makes everything I do actually market research for possibly a product.

Now some things, are just way too complicated, some things I may do inside my business to turn into a product, but then maybe later on I may think of a different way to present it or a different way to do it that does make it easier and then I can show other people how to do that.

Robert: I see you present something at platinum one time and then present it on an Armand Live, saying the exact same thing only a little simpler, until you are finally ready to do it in an actual course, and then it's as few clicks as possible.

Armand: And it's kind of funny that you mention that because a lot of times what happens is I will be teaching something and I will talk to the platinum group, and I will be showing them a strategy and I can pretty much talk openly and explain the strategy and show them step by step of how to do that. But then, I can say the same thing at an Armand Morin Live, where I will have to simplify it down for the majority of the people in the audience. And even after doing that a couple times when I think they have the hang of it, people come up to me privately and ask me, "How did you do this or how did you do that."

I will simplify it again, and then hopefully that will remove those questions and I won't have as many. And then many times, from that point I will turn it into a product. And that is one pathway to create a product.

Robert: It makes sense to me. So we talked about a lot of cool stuff. Armand talked about how you do software, how you do training courses, and how you come up with an idea. Usually it's that you see a hole in the marketplace or you try to do something and either the way to do it isn't easy enough, you make the first iteration of it, and then you try it out on other people, and you become the guinea pig. You see how people implement training, can I make it easier, or how do I use the software?

We talked about how you compete against everyone else who is more complicated or tries to appear more advanced than you. And you said, be the first person to market, the easier to use and have better support, because that applies to if you are doing a mastermind, a seminar, or doing software. It's been great to talk to you and just look inside your head for a little bit and see how things got started, how things have evolved from the seminars into the live streaming, from doing videos at a membership site to now those are live. And then now they are kind of turning into a budding press, a Facebook kind of thing.

If someone wants to, just to know how you are doing, what you are working on what's you next big thing - where should they go?

Armand: They can go to ArmandMorin.com and you will see if we are doing something new and you can also subscribe to our newsletter list.

Your Blog, Membership Site, Email List...
Making Money Online Automatically and...
It's All Done in Under 3 Days

I'll want to get you on the right track to having all this setup within the next 3 days or less:

- Niche & Domain Name
- Blog & Social Proof
- Web Host & Web Page
- Sales Letter & Payment Button
- Email Optin Page
- Membership Site & Drip Content
- Autoresponder Messages
- Traffic

Even in the fancy $2,000... $3,000... even $10,000 courses... teach USELESS skills that are WAY over your head:

- "Now that you have an optin page, I forgot to tell you... you need a blog"
- "Now that you have a blog, I forgot to tell you... you need a sales page"
- "Now that you have a sales page, I forgot to tell you... you need a product"

Sound familiar? Nothing takes you from start to finish... in just one easy weekend, until now:

http://www.IncomeMachine.com

About the Author

Robert Plank runs a million dollar business on the Internet creating information products, software tools, and webinar training.

He can show you how to not only save time in your business and everyday life, but do more in less time. Master WordPress. Build your list. Create passive income from information products. Generate residual income using membership sites. Scale and talk to use audiences using webinars. And more!

Robert's Online Presence:

- Blog: www.robertplank.com
- Podcast: www.robertplankshow.com/itunes
- Fan Page: www.robertplankshow.com

Robert Plank's other titles on Amazon.com:

- 100 Time Savers: Start Less, Finish More, and Cut 10 Minutes a Day from Your Schedule to Gain 60 Hours of Free Time Per Year
- Article Crash Course: Get Published, Get Instant Authority and Become an Expert in Any Subject
- Double Agent Marketing: Live the Double Life, Control Your Destiny and Become a Self-Employed Entrepreneur By Starting Your Own Home-Based Internet Information Business
- Four Daily Tasks: Overcome All Internal Roadblocks Using a Few Simple Rules, Solve Any Personal Problems and Keep Moving in a "Forward" Direction in 10 Easy Steps
- Internet Marketing on Crack: Master Your Time Management, Marketing, Sales, Traffic, Products, Customer Relationships & More From Just a Few Simple Breakthroughs
- List, Traffic & Offers: The Internet Marketing Profit Shortcut
- Membership Cube: How to Create a Passive Income in Just a Few Simple Clicks

- Secret Conversations with Internet Millionaires: How to Make Money Online with an Internet Marketing Business
- Sell on Amazon FBA: Easy Steps to Create an Online Passive Income Amazon Business with Retail Arbitrage & Private Label Sourcing
- Setup a Point & Click Website Today: Install WordPress, Create Massive Content, Secure and Backup Your Blog WITHOUT Being a Computer Geek

Robert's courses:

- Membership Cube: setup a recurring membership site
- Income Machine: establish your online system including your blog, traffic, opt-in page, autoresponder sequence and more
- Dropship CEO: sell physical products on Amazon.com
- Make a Product: self-publish a book (physical and digital) on Amazon.com
- Profit Dashboard: earn money from Fiverr
- Podcast Crusher: create your own podcast

Discover more about him at RobertPlank.com/about and contact him at RobertPlank.com/ask if you have a personal question, want to appear on his podcast, want him on your podcast, or if you wish to enquire about availability for speaking engagements.

www.ingramcontent.com/pod-product-compliance
Lightning Source LLC
Chambersburg PA
CBHW051535170526
45165CB00002B/740